AF573431

Soccer Club Geopolitics

Kévin Veyssière

Soccer Club Geopolitics

22 Unusual Stories to Understand the World

Max Milo

Max Milo, Paris, 2024
www.maxmilo.com
ISBN : 978-2-31502-162-8

Foreword

Kévin Veyssière set up a social networking page, "FC Geopolitics", which quickly became a huge success, attracting the attention of an ever-growing audience. The reasons for this success are very simple: to combine serious documentation with a judicious choice of illustrations. The subjects he tackles arouse curiosity, but are far from anecdotal: they lead to in-depth reflection, all in a pleasant tone. Kévin Veyssière likes to astonish and take us down circuitous paths. He manages to show that soccer is a very serious subject, and that geopolitics can be fun. The little stories are there for the big ones, and he takes us along in an attractive way.

Kévin Veyssière reminds us of the time when Franco's Spain refused to play against the USSR, or how Croatia used its national team to gain international recognition. Closer to home, he evokes the "impossible matches" of the Kosovo team, those that would pit Gibraltar against Spain, or Armenia against Azerbaijan. These can range from the *seemingly* anecdotal (Tuvalu) to the weighty (the Qatar-Saudi Arabia duel). It's always precise and enjoyable.

In the early days of European soccer, before the advent of mass television and social networks, many teenagers learned about

European geography by reading about the results of foreign championships and European cups. No doubt, in a few years' time, many people will say they became interested in geopolitics through Kévin Veyssière's stories, seeking to broaden their knowledge after realizing that no, geopolitics isn't boring and off-putting, and that it's not just for seasoned diplomats and staff officers.

Shortly before the 1998 World Cup, I suggested to two publishers—one academic, the other general public—that I should write a book on the theme of soccer and international relations. They didn't laugh in my face, out of politeness. They didn't think any less of me. Courteously, they made me understand that, since my passion—guilty as charged for an academic—was something as trifling as soccer, I could possibly write a book on the subject. But they urged me to write a book on international relations, since that was my profession and my specialty. They saw absolutely no connection between the two, and gave me friendly advice against pursuing this pipe dream.

Soccer is now less despised by the intellectual elite, and geopolitics is widely rehabilitated. Linking soccer and geopolitics is now a matter of course. Kévin Veyssière illustrates this with talent. He succeeds in opening up the curiosity of soccer fans to geopolitics, and demonstrates to those interested in geostrategic issues that soccer can be part of it.

Pascal Boniface

Introduction

From June 14, 2024, the 17th edition of the Euro will be held, the major international event in European soccer. Soccer again, you may ask? Since its inception in 1960, the Euro has served to break down barriers and ease relations between European nations, already shaken by the two world wars. It's no coincidence that the Union of European Football Associations (UEFA), which was behind the creation of this summer tournament, was born at the same time as the political and economic construction of Europe, with the signing of the Treaties of Rome in 1957. The idea was to reunite the European continent through sport and to find a new arena, other than the battlefield, on which nations could compete.

The gamble seems to have paid off, since today the UEFA organization brings together almost 55 member countries, far more than the European Union (27) or the Council of Europe (47). Football has succeeded in transcending borders, even beyond the continent itself. The Europe of soccer now extends as far as Kazakhstan! Soccer now embraces every stratum of society, revealing the strengths and weaknesses of every state on our planet.

On the sporting field, matches replace the old warlike confrontations, as can be the case when England and Scotland clash. Or they enable nations to make their mark, like Croatia at Euro 1996, who were able to wear their chequered jersey, a national symbol, for the first time in an international soccer competition. A situation that Georgia is about to experience, as its national team takes part in the Euro for the first time, against a backdrop of integration into the European Union.

Indeed, the world's most popular sport is a formidable showcase, synonymous for states with leverage to attract their territory: a *soft power* tool[1], to shine and seduce in the eyes of the world; a source of influence that can be used to bring a country out of anonymity or change its image. This is the path taken by Qatar, which has become a key player in the world of football and sport, particularly since the organization of the 2022 World Cup, which not only put an entire country in the spotlight, but also highlighted its limitations, particularly in terms of human rights. Proof that using sport as a tool to promote one's territory can be a double-edged sword, and ultimately do as much harm as good.

National teams sometimes play such an ambassadorial role that a soccer match can be like a new battle. As when the Hong Kong team's victory over China sparked off riots in Beijing in 1985. Or when Argentina's Diego Maradona "avenged" the Falklands War by defeating England in the 1986 World Cup. In some cases, the situation is such that matches are impossible. Kosovo, whose state existence is not internationally recognized, is one such case. Its national team simply cannot play against certain other countries.

1."Soft power is this soft power, which has become the new and subtle form of power, where each state tries to attract the attention, respect and sympathy of other nations", BONIFACE Pascal, *Géopolitique du sport*, Armand Colin, 2014.

When real war breaks out, soccer has no place as an instrument of peace, as is the case between Armenia and Azerbaijan in the Nagorno-Karabakh region.

Beyond simple encounters between respective countries, soccer can also be the source of great stories to promote a country's autonomy. Like the epic of the "Eleven of Independence" in the 1960s, in their quest for a free Algeria. Practices that are being replicated today in Greenland, a gigantic Danish territory that is seeking a path to independence through football. Thousands of kilometers from the Arctic, Easter Island also uses soccer to promote recognition of the Rapa Nui culture, proving that this sport can enable populations and regions to achieve greater autonomy. Last but not least, soccer can serve as a formidable wake-up call on the urgent issue of global warming, and thus save what can still be saved of the Tuvalu Islands in Oceania.

Far from being exhaustive, this book invites the curious, whether soccer fans or budding geographers, to explore the world through soccer stories and great sporting moments, while helping to understand the political, economic and social issues facing our planet.

Soccer isn't just about the ball.

Kévin Veyssière

Part 1: Europe

I. The Euro Soccer Championship, a History Intimately Linked to that of Europe

1. Euro Soccer in the Footsteps of European Integration

The European Nations Football Championship was born at the same time as the beginnings of European economic and political construction. This was no coincidence, as the decision-makers of the continent's various countries were seeking to unite and avoid repeating the mistakes of previous world wars. In a way, the Euro soccer tournament helped push back the frontiers. The round ball pierced the "Iron Curtain" and enabled the nations of the Western and Eastern blocs to meet on a terrain other than that of the Cold War.

Europe is the birthplace of soccer. The first real club was founded in England in 1857, in the city of Sheffield. It was on English soil that the first international soccer match in history was played, on November 30, 1872, against Scotland. The game was then exported across the continent and around the world by merchants, settlers and representatives of the British Empire. Such was its success that other teams were born. The first match between two non-British national teams took place in Vienna between Austria and Hungary on October 12, 1902. Faced with the internationalization of the *English Game*, teams from across the Channel gradually began to turn in on themselves, presenting themselves as the great patrons of their sport. In fact, the English team collected a string of successes in its first away matches, including a severe 15-0 victory over France in 1906. In other European countries, numerous clubs emerged and organized themselves to counter British hegemony, which was both sporting and political at the time.

Sport, as an instrument for easing international tensions, is also on a roll, since the first modern Olympic Games were created in 1896, on the initiative of Frenchman Pierre de Coubertin. Soccer followed suit. On May 21, 1904, the Fédération Internationale de Football Association, more commonly known today as FIFA, was founded in Paris. The founding members were European: Belgium, Denmark, France, the Netherlands, Spain, Sweden and Switzerland. International matches were confined to friendlies. The benchmark tournament of the time was the Olympic Games, where the British team won the 1908 and 1912 editions. The First World War, from 1914 to 1918, shook the whole of Europe, reshuffling the cards of the powers that be. Not to mention the human disaster that resulted from this terrible conflict, with over 20 million victims.

Sport could have been one of the levers for building a peaceful Europe after the war, but the Versailles Peace Treaty of 1919 shows that the victorious nations were more interested in weakening their rivals than in finding a compromise. This discrepancy was not conducive to the construction of a political Europe. At the same time, new players are competing with European nations at their own game. This was already the case in omnisports, with the United States topping the medals table at the various Olympic Games from 1920 onwards. New nations also made their presence felt in the round ball arena. The Olympic Football Tournament remains the only truly international soccer competition. In 1920, Egypt became the first non-Western team to take part, soon joined by Uruguay in 1924. Uruguay won the tournament against Switzerland that year. The situation was even worse for Europe in 1928, when no European team reached the final! Uruguay won again at the expense of Argentina.

The British nations and Europe no longer have a monopoly on soccer. Above all, FIFA began to give serious thought to the creation of a large-scale international tournament, as the last two Olympic finals had attracted over 30,000 spectators, and it was the highest-grossing soccer competition of all the Olympic events at the time. As part of this development, FIFA allows professional players to take part, as many European countries have already started to set up their own leagues. This did not sit well with the International Olympic Committee (IOC), which wished to preserve the value of amateurism at its Games. This disagreement led to the creation of the first soccer World Cup, in 1930.

The organizer's choice was the hottest team of the moment, Uruguay. Officially to celebrate the country's centenary, unofficially because Uruguay agreed to pay the teams' participation fees and build a new stadium dedicated to the final of this new world competition. Although the Uruguayan team won this first edition, this was not the case for the following ones, which took place in Europe, in 1934 in Italy and in 1938 in France. The soccer craze of those years was not used to bring nations closer together. As evidenced by the organization of the 1934 World Cup in Mussolini's Italy, and the 1936 Olympic Games in Nazi Germany, sport was used to legitimize the dictatorial regimes of the host countries.

However, the idea of creating a European competition was already present, with Henri Delaunay, General Secretary of the French Football Federation, pushing for the organization of an international tournament on the European continent as early as 1927. The creation of the World Cup sounded the death knell for this project. It wasn't until the end of the Second World War that the idea resurfaced, this time with the firm intention of bringing people together through sport, and not making the same mistakes as in the past. At the end of the war, while the "fathers" of Europe (Jean Monnet, Robert Schuman, Paul-Henri Spaak) were working on the economic and political construction of Europe, three other men were developing the continent's sporting union: the Italian Ottorino Barassi, the Belgian José Crahay and the French Henri Delaunay. Things had been moving since 1953, when FIFA lifted the ban on the creation of continental federations. This decision was taken following pressure from European countries in the face of the growing influence of South American nations. The first post-war World Cup, in 1950, ended with Uruguay defeating Brazil. At the same time, soccer was becoming increasingly internationalized, and the influence of Europeans on FIFA's decisions began to wane.

These two trends—countering South American leadership in soccer, and reinforcing the logic of bringing peoples closer together—with the creation of the Council of Europe in 1949 and the European Coal and Steel Community (ECSC) in 1952—gave rise to the idea of creating a European soccer organization. On June 15, 1954, the Union of European Football Associations (UEFA) was founded in the Swiss city of Basel—a federation that went beyond mere politics, as 25 delegates took part, representing 30 soccer federations, including some from the Eastern Bloc. Since the end of the Second World War, Europe has been divided in two by an "Iron Curtain". This expression symbolizes the political border dividing the European continent into two distinct zones: a Western bloc made up of European states oriented towards the USA, and an Eastern bloc made up of European states under the influence of the USSR. Soccer is one of the few ways of blurring this political boundary.

The creation of UEFA should logically have led to the creation of a European competition between the various national teams. While South America's Copa America has existed since 1916, the project for a European equivalent has been slow to materialize. The death in 1954 of Henri Delaunay, one of UEFA's founders, further hampered the project. Meanwhile, clubs were getting organized. Following an article in the *Daily Mirror* in December 1954, which proclaimed that the English club Wolverhampton deserved the title of European champion after two victories over Budapest Honvéd and Spartak Moscow, the French newspaper *L'Équipe* counter-attacked. At the instigation of its journalist Gabriel Hanot, it proposed the creation of a European cup to prove that British hegemony in football was far from a foregone conclusion[2]. It's an idea that ties in with another, as the sports daily has for some years been looking to create a competition to boost its mid-week newspaper sales.

On April 3 1955, the newspaper *L'Équipe* and the presidents of Europe's leading clubs agreed to create the European Champion Clubs' Cup, the forerunner of today's Champions League. The first edition of this European Cup was launched in the 1955-1956 season. If UEFA did not intervene immediately in this matter, it was primarily because Henri Delaunay was no longer in charge, and the

2. Mouton Olivier, *Hors-Jeu. 22 matchs de foot qui ont marqué l'histoire,* Armand Colin, 2017—chap. 6, p. 61.

organization had been created at the outset with the political aim of defending European positions within FIFA, rather than setting up sporting competitions.

The European Cup was so popular (with almost 124,000 spectators in the Santiago-Bernabéu stadium for the 1957 final between Real Madrid and Fiorentina) that the idea of creating a competition between the main national teams resurfaced within the UEFA governing bodies. After much wrangling with FIFA, the principle of a European Nations Championship, or Euro Football Championship, was agreed in June 1958 in Stockholm. A year earlier, the Treaties of Rome had been signed, laying the foundations of the European Economic Community (EEC).

There remained the daunting task of convincing the national federations to take part in this future Euro, to be held between 1958 and 1960. Pierre Delaunay, Henri's son, embarked on a tour to convince 17 national federations to take part in this first competition. As with the European Club Cup, this sporting tournament brought together countries beyond the "Iron Curtain", as even the USSR agreed to take part. The very first match of this championship, or at least the qualifying rounds, took place on September 28, 1958: the USSR met Hungary in Moscow's Central Lenin Stadium, where over 100,000 people turned out to watch the game. Other matches allowed nations from different blocs to meet. Like on April 5, 1959, when the Republic of Ireland, a western nation, met Czechoslovakia, an eastern nation.

As the years go by, the Euro continues to grow and break down borders. For the 2024 edition in Germany, 53 UEFA member national teams are taking part in the qualifiers. 24 teams will compete in the final phase this summer. This makes the "Europe of soccer" an important lever in the construction of Europe as a continent, and even beyond, since national soccer teams such as those of Azerbaijan, Israel and Kazakhstan are also present. In this way, the European Nations Football Championship has achieved its main objective of bringing people together, breaking down barriers and extending European borders.

2. Euro 1960: Franco's Spain Refuses to Play the USSR

The first Euro soccer tournament, in 1960, was a real boon for UEFA, whose ambition was to make its tournament the most watched competition on the planet. However, a decisive match between the two main favorites, Spain and the USSR, turned this sporting moment into a political one. It highlights the major differences between Europe, the ideological divide between the Western and Eastern blocs, and the Cold War.

We left Euro 1960, in the previous chapter, with one of the matches that transcended the European divisions of the Cold War, that between the Republic of Ireland and Czechoslovakia. In this game, it was the team from the East that qualified for the rest of the European Nations Championship. Although the competition features 17 competing nations, some of Europe's top teams, such as England, Germany and Italy, have declined the invitation. The reason: they have doubts about the success of this new tournament. Yet France, third in the 1958 World Cup, Sweden, finalists against Brazil, and Spain, with many Real Madrid players, are all there.

The Madrid-based club is on top of Europe, having won every European Champion Clubs' Cup title since 1956, and boasts some of the best players in the game, most notably Alfredo Di Stéfano. In other words, Spain are the scarecrows of this first Euro. To reach the final phase of the competition, the teams involved must still play two rounds of knockout matches, a sort of round of 16 and quarter-finals before their time. The main favourites have no trouble distinguishing themselves during their warm-up rounds. UEFA, the competition's organizers, can keep smiling.

In the next round, a shadow slipped over the table. The USSR team, who easily overcame Hungary, meet Spain in the quarter-finals. A mouth-watering match on paper, between the two footballing forces of the moment. The Soviets won the soccer event at the 1956 Olympic Games in Melbourne. But the match never took place. Because of one man: Franco. The military dictator had ruled Spain since 1939. To achieve this, he had to win the Spanish Civil War between 1936 and 1939, during which the USSR supported the People's Army of the Spanish Republic, while Fascist Italy and Nazi Germany lent their support to Franco's nationalist regime.

The "Caudillo", Franco's nickname, kept this "betrayal" in mind. Nine days before the first leg, a Council of Ministers meeting was held to decide whether the Spanish team should play the Soviet team at Euro 1960. Four days later, the final decision was made. It was decided that the Spanish team would not play the USSR. The decision was justified in writing by the fact that Spanish soldiers from the Azul Division, who had been made available by Spain to the Wehrmacht during the Second World War to fight on the Russian front, were still being held prisoner in the Siberian gulags.

Just before leaving for the match, the Spanish team remained grounded. Legend has it that Spanish star Di Stéfano lamented:

"Why? Why?" he said to a federation official. "Why? Franco's orders"[3], was the reply. It has to be said that the military general took a very dim view of the fact that the Spanish team could suffer defeat in Moscow, and thus deal a direct blow to the legitimacy and effectiveness of his political regime. The old demons of the Spanish Civil War could also have resurfaced if "Soviet ambassadors" in spikes had come to the capital Madrid.

In any case, this decision is terrible for UEFA, which does not want the political decisions of its member countries to interfere with the smooth running of its competition, which is presented as apolitical. The newspapers, for their part, were quick to draw the line. Agence France-Presse headlined: "Football is a victim of the Cold War".[4] UEFA then tried everything and proposed a compromise. The match would be played on neutral ground. The Spanish regime accepted, but the Soviets refused. The European soccer governing body had no choice but to abdicate and announce the USSR's qualification. Spain, excluded, was fined 2,000 Swiss francs. The great Spanish generation of the time, who dominated European soccer with Real Madrid, lost the opportunity to win a major international title. Particularly Di Stéfano, who never won a title with Spain.

On the Soviet side, the team has the privilege of taking part in the first ever Euro soccer finals. For this part of the competition between the last four qualifying teams, matches are no longer played over two legs, but in a knockout format. UEFA chooses France to host the final round, in tribute to Henri Delaunay. This did not bring Les

3. Mouton Olivier, *Hors-Jeu. 22 matchs de foot qui ont marqué l'histoire,* Armand Colin, 2017—chap. 8, p. 83.
4. Mouton Olivier, *Hors-Jeu. 22 matchs de foot qui ont marqué l'histoire,* Armand Colin, 2017—chap. 8, p. 84.

Bleus any luck, as they lost to Yugoslavia in the semi-finals, while the USSR defeated Czechoslovakia.

The final on July 10, 1960 at the Parc des Princes stadium in Paris had all the makings of a political encounter. Now a leader of the non-aligned movement, Yugoslavia, governed by General Tito, had severed relations with the USSR since 1948. A Yugoslav victory would be seen as a triumph on the Soviet model. All the more so as the players were promised a plot of land in the event of victory. However, in the decisive match, legendary Soviet goalkeeper Lev Yashin tamed the Balkan offensives, and it was striker Viktor Ponedelnik who propelled the "Red Army" to the summit of European soccer. A victory that brings relief.

The USSR had already crossed paths with Yugoslavia at the 1952 Olympic soccer tournament in Helsinki. The Yugoslav victory angered Stalin, who severely punished the team's players and coach. By 1960, honor had been restored. With this sporting victory, the Soviet regime could boast that its political model had prevailed over all others, particularly those of the West. All the more so as the final podium of this first Euro crowned three national teams from Eastern Europe: the USSR, Yugoslavia and Czechoslovakia.

Is Franco biting his fingers? History doesn't tell us. Meanwhile, most Spanish players were comforted by another European title for Real Madrid, with a 7-3 victory over Eintracht Frankfurt. Proof that Spain is on top form, the 1960 Ballon d'Or was awarded to FC Barcelona's Luis Suarez. But the golden generation did not lose everything. Franco had his revenge four years later, at the second edition of the Euro in 1964.

This time, Spain qualified for the finals, and even offered to organize them. A fine opportunity to showcase Franco and his political regime. However, UEFA imposed a condition on the tournament being played on Spanish soil. The USSR team, also qualified, must be allowed to take part. European leaders are keen to avoid a further setback, especially as the competition has grown in stature, with 27 teams taking part in the qualifying rounds.

The final phase took place in Spain, pitting the host nation against Denmark, Hungary and, of course, the USSR. While the Soviets easily qualified for the final, Spain almost missed out, needing a final goal in extra time to defeat the Hungarian team. The long-awaited match took place on June 21, 1964.

In front of almost 80,000 people in Madrid's boiling Santiago Bernabéu stadium, and above all in front of Franco himself, the Roja players simply had no room for error. The match began with a bang. Barcelona's Jesús Perada opened the scoring in the 6th minute. Two minutes later, Spartak Moscow striker Galimzian Khoussaïnov replied. Lev Yachine, once again, kept the opposition at bay, but it was the Spaniard Marcelino who finally enabled this great Spanish team to win its first international title.

A consecration for Spanish soccer, but also for Franco, who was looking for another major sporting victory, in addition to Real Madrid's European Cup triumph, to raise his profile on the international stage. The 1964 Euro triumph was the only achievement of the Spanish team under Franco's regime. It wasn't until the 1990s, and above all the historic treble of Euro, World Cup and Euro from 2008 to 2012, that Spain's soccer once again shone.

3. When Geopolitics Reshuffles the Euro 1992 Deck

In 1992, the Euro was to crown one of the main favourites—English, German, French or Dutch. But the tournament was thrown into turmoil by the collapse of the USSR and the Balkan wars. A surprise guest caused a sensation: Denmark, who took advantage of the exclusion of a Yugoslavia in the midst of conflict to reveal themselves to the eyes of the continent and write one of the finest pages in the history of European soccer.

Euro 1992 was a double event: on the one hand, it was the first European Championship of soccer nations after the fall of the USSR; on the other, it defied all predictions, with Denmark as the unexpected winner. This triumph would not have been possible without the many geopolitical upheavals of the period. The early 1990s ushered in a new era for Europe. The fall of the Berlin Wall on November 9, 1989 symbolized the end of the "Iron Curtain" political frontier in Europe, bringing down the various communist regimes in the East.

The end of the bipolar world gave Europe an opportunity to regain a central role in global decision-making. And it didn't wait for this to happen, since since the late 1980s, European countries have been seeking to federate. This began with the Single European Act of 1986, which paved the way for a European market and a common approach to foreign policy, soon followed by the Maastricht Treaty of 1992, establishing the European Union.

Soccer was one of the playgrounds of the time, helping us to understand these various upheavals. The 1992 European Nations Championship in Sweden saw the qualification of the Soviet Union's soccer team, which posed a problem since the USSR officially disappeared on December 26, 1991. It was initially replaced by the Commonwealth of Independent States (CIS), an intergovernmental entity made up of ten former Soviet republics. The former USSR team was allowed to take part in Euro 1992 under the CIS banner for one competition, before the team disappeared to make way for the national teams of the newly independent countries.

As the last vestige of the Soviet Empire prepares to play its final soccer tournament, the Balkan region is ablaze with the break-up of Yugoslavia. This federation of multi-ethnic republics came into being in 1945. After following the Soviet communist model for a time, the Federal Republic broke with the USSR and maintained a policy of neutrality during the Cold War. Tito, the leader of Yugoslavia, was instrumental in extricating the country from Stalin's influence. He described Yugoslavia as a federation "made up of six republics, five nations, four languages, three religions, two alphabets and a single party". When he died in 1980, after thirty-five years in power, the Yugoslav structure began to crumble, with the rise of nationalism in the various federated republics, long held in check by central government.

The collapse of the USSR accelerated demands for greater autonomy, particularly in Eastern Europe, where many Communist regimes, satellites of Moscow, were overthrown. Yugoslavia was no exception, with two of its federated republics, Slovenia and Croatia, declaring independence in 1991. The Yugoslav state was quick to retaliate, and the Balkan wars began. While the conflict with Slovenia lasted just ten days, the wars in Croatia and then Bosnia were protracted, as Slobodan Milošević's Republic of Serbia sought to aggressively integrate the Serbian minorities in these countries into its territory. It was the conflict with Bosnia that led to the exclusion of the Yugoslav soccer team from Euro 1992.

The cause? Following the international community's recognition of Bosnia's independence on April 6, 1992, Yugoslavia counter-attacked and bombed the Bosnian capital, Sarajevo. United Nations sanctions soon followed, with the adoption of Resolution 757 on May 30, 1992. This brought with it a wide range of sanctions, including the obligation for UN member states to prevent athletes representing the Federal Republic of Yugoslavia from taking part in sporting events on their territory. The following day, May 31 1992, FIFA's emergency committee immediately decided to suspend the Yugoslav federation, soon followed by UEFA, which excluded the Yugoslav team from the European Nations Championship due to start on June 10 in Sweden.

Ten days before the start of the competition, we learn that one of the main favourites will not be taking part in this great footballing celebration. This was a major blow for the team, whose ranks included a number of players who had won the 1991 European Champion Clubs' Cup with Red Star Belgrade: Siniša Mihajlović, Robert Prosinečki, Dejan Savićević and Darko Pančev, among others. Despite a golden generation, the Yugoslav national team was beginning to follow the same path as its war-torn homeland. Coach Ivica Osim and captain Faruk Hadžibegić, both Bosnians, had already packed their bags following the Serbian army's offensive on their homeland.

With Yugoslavia excluded, Denmark, second in their qualifying group, took part in Euro 1992. A funny situation, considering that at the same time, the Danes voted 50.7% against the Maastricht Treaty, the founding act of the European Union. At the same time, Danish players voted yes to one of Europe's major sporting competitions. Legend has it that the Danish national team learned the news while the entire squad was on vacation. It's an image that will stick with the players throughout the competition, described as sportsmen who have come to Sweden with flip-flops on their feet, wives on their arms and beers in their pockets.

But this scenario is far from the truth. Player Kim Vilfort commented: "A week before, we played a game against the CIS and came away with a 1-1 draw. The internationals who were playing abroad then went on vacation. But during the three days that brought us together for this match, we learned that it was possible to be drafted. We knew that.[5] An announcement that nevertheless postponed the plans of Danish coach Richard Møller Nielsen, who had planned to remodel his kitchen that summer. The Danes then embarked on a commando training camp lasting a few days to get back into the rhythm of the competition. Player John Sivebæk recalls "what a mess it was. During the first few training sessions, the team wasn't in great shape. There were quite a few differences between those who had just finished the season and those who had just come back from vacation"[6].

---

5. GHEMMOUR Chérif, Pedro Alexandre, "Il était une fois Richard-Moller Niesen et le Danemark 1992", *So Foot*, February 2014.
6. *Ibid.*

In addition to this truncated preparation, the Danish national team is off to a very poor start: its stars of the day, the brothers Michael and Brian Laudrup, have been absent from the team since 1990, and the coach's choices are contested. The *Danish Dynamite*, the team's nickname, are a shadow of their former selves. To top it all off, Denmark have inherited the most complicated group. Their opponents are France, unbeaten in their qualifying matches, England, third at the 1990 World Cup, and hosts Sweden.

The Danes got their Euro off to the worst possible start. In two games, they failed to score a single goal, managed a miraculous draw against England and lost to neighboring Sweden, thanks to a Tomas Brolin goal. With France's destiny in their own hands, Les Bleus were stunned by Denmark. A goal from Lars Elstrup gave the Danes a 2-1 win and a place in the semi-finals.

The fairytale continues. In the semi-final, the underdogs take on the defending champions, the Netherlands. After a hard-fought battle, the two teams had to go through a penalty shoot-out to decide the winner. Goalkeeper Peter Schmeichel's save from a shot by Dutch star Marco Van Basten propelled the Danish team into the final. For the final showdown, the opponents were the 1990 World Cup winners, Germany. This is not just any German team, as it is the first reunited German team since the fall of the Berlin Wall and the disappearance of the East German team on September 12, 1990. A victory at the Euro would symbolically seal the reunification of Germany, proclaimed on October 3, 1990.

And yet, right from the start, it was Denmark's prolific midfielder, John "Faxe" Jensen, who opened the scoring with his only shot on target of the tournament! Proof that this goal was exceptional was the fact that, prior to this match, the midfielder had only scored once in 48 appearances. Kim Vilfort finished off the job to give Denmark a 2-0 win. He had to leave his team-mates during the competition to be with his daughter, who was suffering from leukemia—she unfortunately lost her battle with the disease a few days later.

On June 26, 1992, in the Gothenburg stadium, surprise guest Denmark won their first-ever European Football Championship. As Vilfort points out, Denmark "didn't have the best players, but they certainly had the best team". The team's nonchalance portrayed by the media was just a facade, as captain Lars Olsen reports: "When we were on the pitch, we were focused and serious, but off it we could have fun, and we did." The day after the victory, the press headlined: "Denmark says yes to the Euro". A premonitory headline, since after the Edinburgh agreements, which defined exceptions for Denmark, a second referendum was held in 1993. The Danes said yes to Europe for a second time, agreeing to join the European Union.

4. When Euro 1996 Helped Croatia Gain International Recognition

In the early 1990s, the Yugoslav wars broke out, exacerbating tensions between the Croatian and Serbian populations of this federation. As Croatia sought independence, its soccer team offered an opportunity to promote the future symbols of its sovereignty and to draw international attention to its situation. This culminated in Croatia's first participation in an international soccer competition, Euro 1996, before the "team with the checkered flag" pulled off a surprise at the 1998 World Cup in France.

While we've left Denmark on top of Europe, the situation in the Balkans is getting worse. By the early 1990s, relations between the various republics of the Yugoslav federation had been deteriorating for almost a decade. Since the creation of the Federal Republic of Yugoslavia in 1945, following the end of the Second World War, the country's unity has been maintained with an iron fist by the authoritarian leader Josip Broz Tito. A situation that inspired this metaphor from General de Gaulle: "There are only pieces of wood that hold [Yugoslavia] together because they are tied to a piece of string. The piece of string is Tito. When he's gone, the pieces of wood will scatter."[7] The general had a point, for when Tito died in 1980, nationalism reared its ugly head in the six republics of Yugoslavia: Slovenia, Croatia, Bosnia, Serbia, Montenegro and Macedonia.

In the early 1980s, secessionist movements by Albanian minorities emerged in Kosovo, then an autonomous province of Yugoslavia, and in Serbia. Demonstrations were severely repressed. On the Slovenian and Croatian sides, both sides sought greater autonomy within the federation. This was not to the liking of Yugoslavia's new strongman, President Slobodan Milošević of the Republic of Serbia, who wanted to preserve the federation's unity while promoting strong Serbian nationalism. The divorce was finalized in January 1990, when the Croatian and Slovenian delegations left the congress of the League of Communists of Yugoslavia.

A few months later, free elections were scheduled in both countries. In Slovenia, Milan Kučan of the Democratic Reform Party wins the election. In Croatia, Franjo Tuđman's Croatian Democratic Union (HDZ) won on May 6, 1990. The atmosphere on Croatian soil was more electric than in Slovenia. A majority of Croats wanted Croatia to leave the Yugoslav federation and become a sovereign country. At the same time, many ethnic Serbs living on Croatian soil opposed secession and wanted their territory to remain attached to Serbia. This tension materialized a week later, on May 13, 1990, during a soccer match between Dinamo Zagreb and Red Star Belgrade. The match, scheduled to take place in Zagreb's Maksimir stadium, did not go ahead. Pre-match clashes between Dinamo's Bad Blue Boys and Red Star's Delije supporters degenerated into

7. GHEMMOUR Chérif, *Terrain Miné, quand la politique s'immisce dans le soccer*, Hugo Sport, 2013, p. 135.

rioting. After the Serbian fans began attacking their counterparts with cries of "Zagreb is Serbian" and "We'll kill Tuđman"[8], the Croatian fans counterattacked; the stadium was invaded and the match became the scene of a veritable battlefield.

In the midst of this chaos, several Dinamo players remained on the pitch, including captain Zvonimir Boban, who kicked a Serbian policeman to protect a Croatian supporter: "There I was, a public figure ready to risk my life, my career and everything that fame could have brought, for an ideal, a cause: the Croatian cause."[9] A kick that would become a symbol of Croatian resistance against Serbia. The "official" toll was heavy: 138 injured and 147 arrested. The non-match had several consequences: Boban was suspended by the Yugoslav Football Federation for six months, which meant he missed the World Cup in the summer of 1990, depriving the national team of one of its greatest hopes.

More importantly, this confrontation is seen internationally as the symbol of ethnic tensions in Yugoslavia. It has been dubbed "the kick-off to the Balkan war". As Loïc Trégourès, professor of political science and author of the book *Le Football dans le chaos Ygoslave*[10], puts it, "the incidents at Maksimir served to illustrate the irreversible nature of the split within Yugoslavia". The match was the umpteenth spark to ignite the already burning nationalist embers in a tense political context. To this day, the match remains for the Croatians a founding event of their nation. A plaque at the entrance to the Zagreb stadium pays tribute to "the team's supporters who, on this pitch, started the war against Serbia on May 13 1990".

8. *Ibid*, p. 139.
9. Ghemmour Chérif, "Le jour où Boban a réalisé son *high kick*", *So Foot*, May 2020.
10. Trégourès Loïc, *Football in the chaos of Yugoslavia*, Non Lieu, 2019.

The Maksimir stadium was once again the scene of Croatian nationalism on June 3, 1990. The Yugoslav team faced the Netherlands in front of a hostile crowd. The Yugoslav anthem was booed. Spectators chanted: "Croatia! Croatia!" The captain at the time, Faruk Hadžibegić even says, "Tonight, we're 11 against 20,000."[11]

The stadium still plays a key role in Croatia's first representation as a national entity. On October 17, 1990, a match took place between a selection of Yugoslav players and the United States team, then on tour in Europe. At least, that's what it said on paper. Unofficially, however, the team present against the Americans was indeed a genuine Croatian team. Whether it's the chequered shirts (the historic coat of arms of the medieval kingdom of Croatia), the anthems played, the banners in the stadium or even the match ticket which clearly states "Croatia/United States". The team looks good, featuring players selected for the Yugoslavian national team, such as midfielder Aljoša Asanović and goalkeeper Dražen Ladić. For Croatian soccer, this first match is considered the very first international match for the *Vatreni, the* team's nickname. The match was followed by another in December 1990, against Romania, in which the young Croatian talents of the time, Zvonimir Boban, Robert Jarni and Davor Šuker, all played. For its part, FIFA did everything in its power not to make these matches official, in order to avoid offending the Yugoslav federation and setting a political precedent that could give ideas to other nations seeking independence.

However, the first official Croatian national team did not see the light of day immediately. On May 19, 1991, Croatia held a referendum in which 93% of voters voted in favor of independence. The

11. *Ibid*, pp. 58-59.

decision was contested by Slobodan Milošević and, a month later, the People's Army of Yugoslavia invaded the country, starting the Croatian War. A ceasefire came into effect in January 1992, with the recognition of Croatia as a sovereign state by the international community. This led to Croatia's eventual admission to FIFA and UEFA. However, this late admission did not allow Croatia to take part in the qualifying rounds for the 1994 World Cup. The first official match recognized by FIFA took place on September 4, 1994, with a victory over Estonia.

On the battlefield, after a final Croatian offensive, the war came to an end with the signing of the Erdut Agreement on November 12, 1995. The following year, Euro 1996 was a great opportunity for this new country to show itself to the whole of Europe. The Croatian national team easily qualified for the competition, finishing in first place in their group, level on points with Italy, finalists at the last World Cup. These good results were confirmed at the Euro 1996 finals, when Croatia qualified for the quarter-finals after a convincing 3-0 victory over Denmark, the reigning European champions. The German team put an end to the Croatian adventure, but the most important thing was to put Croatia on the map. As player Igor Štimac said at the time: "We were ambassadors for our country. It was very important that there were Croatian players all over Europe to pass on this message, because with us was Croatia and the Croatian flag."[12]

The Croatian national team would make a much bigger splash two years later, at the 1998 World Cup, where they upset hosts France in the semi-finals. However, after a memorable brace from Lilian Thuram, the Croatian team lost and finished a surprising

12. *Ibid*, pp. 147-148.

third in their first World Cup. Although this success was a tremendous media showcase for the young country, Croatia remained diplomatically isolated until the death of its leader, Franjo Tuđman, in 1999, before taking steps to be fully integrated into Europe on a terrain other than soccer.

5. England-Scotland: the "Brexit Battle"

On June 18, 2021, British rivals England and Scotland will face off in London's Wembley Stadium in the first round of Euro 2021. This match will be more than just a game of soccer, as relations between Scotland and England have become so strained following the Brexit, formalising the UK's exit from the European Union in 2020. Since then, the Scots have felt aggrieved by this decision and wish to leave the British kingdom to join the EU. Could this summer's duel accelerate the process of Scottish independence?[13]

"My friends in the *Tartan Army* [nickname for Scottish fans] are adamant that if Gary McAllister had scored that penalty, Scotland would have won and the whole country would have demanded a vote for independence straight away."[14] This is how Mark Perryman, author of the book *Ingerland: Travels with a Football Nation*[15], describes the atmosphere surrounding the England-Scotland

13. Chapter written for the 1st edition of the book, published before Euro 2021.
14. Nakrani Sachin, "Golden goal: Paul Gascoigne for England *v.* Scotland (1996)", *The Guardian,* December 2014.
15. Perryman Marc, *Ingerland: Travels With a Football Nation,* Simon & Schuster, 2006.

match at Euro 1996. History is set to repeat itself at the 2021 edition of the European Nations Championship, once again highlighting the sporting rivalry between these two countries, which has never been far removed from the political arena.

The question of Scottish independence will be at the heart of the game, as this issue has recently resurfaced. It has to be said that, while the UK did indeed leave the European Union in 2020, the Scots voted over 60% against Brexit in the 2016 referendum. As a reminder, the UK is made up of four constituent nations: England, Scotland, Wales and Northern Ireland. The latter three have devolved administrations, giving them relative autonomy, each with their own government and parliament. This explains why a majority of Scots want to question the decision to leave the EU: why not become a state in its own right again?

Before turning to the question of independence, it's worth looking back at the origins of this historical-sporting rivalry. In the past, England and Scotland have often been the best of enemies. It all began with William the Conqueror's conquest of England in the mid-11th century, when he and his successors had to intervene on Scotland's borders to stop attacks on the north of the country. Eventually, England and Scotland became two distinct kingdoms in the Middle Ages, alternating between phases of peace and war. In the 13th and 14th centuries, the English kingdom sought to acquire its neighbor's lands, leading to the Scottish Wars of Independence. These expansionist ambitions forced Scotland to sign a defensive alliance treaty with France in 1295, known as the "Old Alliance" (*Auld Alliance*).

After a long struggle, James VI, King of Scotland, also became King of England in 1603, creating a personal union between the two kingdoms. Although they shared the same head of state, the two countries were still sovereign and distinct. A century later, however, the Acts of Union of 1707 transformed this union into a single state, the Kingdom of Great Britain, marking the forthcoming birth of the United Kingdom. Over the centuries, Scottish nationalism grew, and eventually Scotland regained greater autonomy with the Scotland Act of 1998, which established a Scottish Parliament for the first time since 1707.

This rivalry was orchestrated throughout the 20th century, particularly through sporting events. England and Scotland are the birthplaces of modern soccer. In fact, it was between these two nations that the very first international soccer match took place, on November 30, 1872, at Hamilton Crescent stadium, in the Glasgow suburb of Partick. Numerous matches served to highlight Scottish nationalism against England, with victory often representing a way of dominating the other, as in the days of the Anglo-Scottish wars. As the matches progress, old antagonisms resurface, as the English team is nicknamed by Scottish supporters the *Auld Enemy*, in other words the enemy of the ancient Franco-Scottish alliance of the Middle Ages that preserved independence.

Despite being smaller and less populous than their English neighbors, Scotland impressed on their debut, recording 10 wins in their first 16 matches against the *Three Lions*. In all, the two teams have played each other more than 114 times, with England so far enjoying a slight advantage with 48 wins, compared with 41 for Scotland, and 25 draws. However, the development of international soccer and the decline of Scottish soccer have somewhat reduced the number of direct confrontations between these two teams. The footballing rivalry has also shifted, with matches against Germany and Argentina (see chapter 17) now considered more important for England than the historic rivalry with

Scotland. Today, the sporting duel between the Rose and the Thistle is more in evidence.

However, a number of matches in recent decades have brought the rivalry back to life. In particular, the match of June 15, 1996 at Wembley Stadium, London, during the European Nations Championship. This Euro was organized by England, even though the national team was moribund. They had just missed out on Euro 92 and the 1994 World Cup. The pressure was clearly on the English side, as the press at the time was expecting the Three Lions to do well. On the fans' side, hopes were high, as evidenced by the popular success of the song *It's Coming Home* by The Lightning Seeds. It rekindled the hopes of a whole nation of soccer fans, who were hoping for the return of a major trophy (the last dating back to the 1966 World Cup) to the birthplace of the game.

As luck would have it, Britain's best enemies were drawn in the same group for this Euro. Rumors were circulating at the time, however, that UEFA did not want them to be drawn together, for fear that the vociferous English and Scottish fans would come to blows. Indeed, the match is already a crucial one for the rest of the competition. Both teams started the Euro with a draw, England against Switzerland and Scotland against the Netherlands. This duel therefore already has all the makings of a decisive match, as defeat would eject either of these two teams from the Euro.

From the stands, Wembley Stadium, with its 70,000 spectators, is in meltdown. The Scottish national anthem, *Flower of Scotland*, is completely drowned out by the booing of the fans. With the game hotly contested, England striker Alan Shearer broke the deadlock in the 53rd minute. Just 15 minutes later, *Three Lions* defender Tony Adams clipped Scottish striker Gordon Durie. With the whole stadium holding its breath, goalkeeper David Seaman turned

Gary McAllister's penalty into a corner. Seconds later, the England counter-attack allowed the whimsical Paul Gascoigne to pull off a sumptuous sombrero kick before crucifying goalkeeper Andy Goram with a right-footed finish. 2-0 to England. A liberation for the whole team, and a fine response from "Gazza", who had been the target of the English tabloids after his extrasporting debacles, notably a drunken outing with several other players during the training camp in Hong Kong.

After this match, both British teams could still qualify for the rest of the competition, but Scotland was ultimately eliminated on goal difference. However, in the final group match, England had their neighbor's fate in their own hands, after leading the Netherlands 4-0. However, a "late" goal from the Dutch side brought the score to 4-1 and eliminated Scotland from the competition. The *Guardian* newspaper reported that, after the match, "England fans were ecstatic when Dutch player Patrick Kluivert scored the goal to deny Scotland a place in the quarter-finals"[16].

This match was not the only notable encounter between the two teams. England and Scotland met again in a double play-off for Euro 2000, on November 13 and 17, 1999, in a duel dubbed by the press "the Battle of Britain". The first leg, at Glasgow's Hampden Park, was the first game the two teams had played in Scotland for almost ten years. England win 2-0, thanks to midfielder Paul Scholes, while the battle between the fans around the stadium rages on. The return leg in London put the Three Lions in doubt, as the Scottish team tried their best, but only managed a 1-0 victory. This was not enough to prevent England from qualifying for Euro 2000—for the record, they went out in the first round.

---

16. Gibbons Michael, "The cultural resonance of Euro 96", *The Guardian*, July 2016.

Although the two teams have met since then, the match on June 18, 2021, at London's Wembley stadium, will be the first duel between England and Scotland in a major soccer competition since 2016. A duel that has all the makings of being the next "Battle of Britain". Could the outcome of the match influence the question of Scottish independence? The subject is certainly a hot one. It's true that the last referendum on this subject saw the No camp win on September 18, 2014 with 55% of the vote. In 2021, in the post-Brexit context, the situation is very different.

Scotland's political powers are already organizing themselves accordingly. On January 25, Nicola Sturgeon, leader of the Scottish Nationalist Party (SNP), unveiled her roadmap to independence: "I want a legal referendum, which is why I'm going to appeal to the authority of the Scottish people in May. And if they give me that authority, I will act accordingly."[17]

It has to be said that, despite the trade agreement reached following the Brexit, Scotland feels it has been wronged on many points, particularly fishing. The Brexit complicates exports from this country, which is Europe's leading salmon producer, and which is now deprived of the advantages of the European market. If the Scottish national team wins this summer, it will be interesting to see whether a sporting event of this magnitude can precipitate a referendum and, after the European Union, a new divorce for the United Kingdom.

17. Brooks Libby, "Sturgeon: SNP will hold Scottish independence vote if it wins in May", *The Guardian*, January 2021.

6. North Macedonia: Historic Participation in Euro 2021

In 2021, a newcomer took part in its very first Euro soccer tournament: North Macedonia. A historic milestone, as it is the first time this young nation has taken part in the competition. The Balkan country is set to become even more integrated into the European sporting family, before, why not, joining the European Union.

"The dream has come true.[18] These were the words of Macedonian soccer star Goran Pandev, scorer of the only goal in North Macedonia's victory over Georgia on November 12, 2020. This success enabled the team to take part in the Euro. It is quite simply the first time in its young history that the Macedonian national team has qualified for a major international soccer tournament. This Euro 2021 was thus an opportunity to showcase a country that has the particularity of being new on the international scene, since Northern Macedonia has only recently taken on this name, following the resolution of a diplomatic dispute with Greece.

18. Rédaction, "Football: a united North Macedonia celebrates its Euro qualification", *Le Courrier des Balkans*, November 2020.

To better understand why this change has taken place, we need to look back a little.

Macedonia is best known for Alexander the Great. Crowned King of Macedonia at the age of 20 and victorious in numerous battles, he conquered an immense empire in ancient times, stretching from Greece to the gates of India. Throughout history, Macedonia has been a region of variable geometry, losing its prestige until it finally lost its independence. At the beginning of the 20th century, the modern territory of Macedonia, under Ottoman domination, became the object of covetousness between Albania, Bulgaria, Greece and Serbia. Several movements pushed for Macedonian independence, but between the beginning of the 20th century and the Second World War, the territory came under Bulgarian and then Serbian domination, before becoming part of the Kingdom of Yugoslavia.

In December 1944, the Anti-Fascist Assembly for the Liberation of the Macedonian People (ASNOM) founded the first Socialist Republic of Macedonia, which was later integrated into the six republics of the federal Yugoslav state. From the 1980s onwards, the unity of Yugoslavia began to crumble. At that time, the Yugoslav state lost its historic leader, Tito, whose authoritarianism had helped to contain the various nationalisms in the federal republic (see chapter 4). The gradual collapse of the USSR and its Eastern bloc in 1991 triggered this process within Yugoslavia. Successive declarations of independence by the former socialist republics of Slovenia and Croatia precipitated the collapse of the federation. Northern Macedonia followed suit, holding a referendum that approved self-determination by over 95%. On September 8, 1991, the Republic of Macedonia was proclaimed.

To become fully integrated into the international scene, the new country quickly tried to join the United Nations. This is where *the* problem arises: the country's name is contested by Greece. This is because the Greek state claims exclusive use of the term Macedonia for the northern province of its territory. A land and a name, as we have seen, steeped in history and bearing the myth of Alexander the Great. For Greece, if a state bears the name Macedonia, it means that the integrity of Greek territory is threatened.

An initial solution was found, with North Macedonia joining the UN in 1993, under the provisional name of the Former Yugoslav Republic of Macedonia (FYROM). This compromise did not suit Greece, which imposed a blockade on Macedonian territory from 1994. Sanctions were finally lifted in September 1995, following conciliation under UN auspices. Macedonia changed various aspects of its constitution and certain elements of its flag, thus removing any ambiguity with Greek claims. The name dispute was finally resolved much later. On June 17, 2018, FYROM and Greece signed the Prespa Agreement, ushering in a new era for the Macedonian country. It officially renamed itself the Republic of North Macedonia on February 12, 2019. The end of the diplomatic dispute lifts the Greek diplomatic veto. A godsend for this "new country", which can now join the major international organizations. This is the case with the NATO Euro-Atlantic alliance on March 27, 2020. And why not soon join the European Union? North Macedonia has been an official candidate for membership since 2004, and its government has made this goal a strategic priority.

This international spotlight will continue since, as we said, the Macedonian soccer team validated its ticket to its first Euro on November 12, 2020, with a victory over Georgia. A historic qualification for a country more accustomed to seeing its basketball and handball teams take center stage. Since joining FIFA and UEFA in 1994, the Macedonian national team, nicknamed the *Crveni*

Lavovi ("Red Lions"), has hardly ever made the headlines. The Euro is therefore a great opportunity to showcase a small country of 25,000 km2 and 2 million inhabitants.

The team's qualification against Georgia also served to rally the Macedonian population around the common national symbol that a soccer team can represent. Jubilant scenes abounded throughout Northern Macedonia, and the country's national anthem echoed through the streets of the capital Skopje. These images of unity are welcome news for a country that has experienced stormy relations with its Albanian minority. The Balkan wars of the 1990s heightened tensions between Macedonians of Slavic and Albanian origin. The war in Kosovo led to the immigration of almost 360,000 Albanian refugees into the country. In 2001, veterans of the war launched a guerrilla war to annex the Albanian regions of Macedonia (the Albanian minority represents around 25% of the Macedonian population) and integrate them into the new Kosovar territory. International mediation brought the conflict to an end, with the signing of the Ohrid Accords on August 13, 2001, which gave greater political power and cultural recognition to the Albanian minority, and made Albanian one of the country's two official languages, alongside Macedonian.

Northern Macedonia's footballing success has united the country across all divides, as half the players on the national team are from the Albanian minority. As Goran Pandev puts it: "We won for our people and for all of us. This message of unity is also echoed by the country's Prime Minister, Zoran Zaev: "Macedonians, Albanians, Turks... under the same jersey, under the same flag, for the common homeland."[19] This is proof that the North Macedonian

19. *Ibid.*

soccer team will have more than just a sporting role to play during the Euro. Its role will be that of ambassador for the country, conveying positive values about the country, far removed from the region's ethnic conflicts.

As Darko Pančev, a former Yugoslav and Macedonian soccer star, once said, "this generation of players has a unique opportunity to succeed and play against the best teams in Europe". Northern Macedonia's journey through the tournament, marked by fierce resistance, was ultimately unsuccessful. However, their participation is a good illustration of how large-scale international tournaments such as Euro 2021 can be used to promote a "new" country and offer moments of national pride and unity.

In any case, North Macedonia's fight for its full integrity is not over, as Bulgaria recently put forward a historical and linguistic dispute to justify its veto in talks between the Macedonian country and the European Union. Will the round ball enable North Macedonia to gain full recognition on the international stage? It's hard to say. In any case, the Euro and its thousands of television viewers remain an important window of exposure for highlighting the particularities of little-known countries, just waiting to shine on the European stage.

II. Impossible Matches

7. Russia-Ukraine

Since 2014 and Russia's annexation of the Ukrainian peninsula of Crimea, relations between the two countries have reached a new stage in terms of tensions. On February 24, 2022, the situation descended into all-out war with Russia's military offensive on Ukrainian territory. UEFA, which had already banned the two national teams from meeting, sided with international sporting sanctions by excluding Russia from its organization. However, while Ukraine will be present at Euro 2024 with its national team, the Russian authorities are trying to be rehabilitated by world soccer organizations. A battle that is more than symbolic in this conflict where every move is allowed.

Before the start of the War in Ukraine in February 2022, the conflict was already present with the annexation of Crimea, a Ukrainian territory, by Russia in March 2014. Given the inherent tensions between the two countries, UEFA had taken the lead on July 17, 2014, by banning all matches between Russian and Ukrainian national teams or clubs in its competitions "In view of the current political situation, the Russian and Ukrainian federations have expressed their concern about safety in the event that

Russian and Ukrainian teams should play each other in UEFA competitions."[20] This is because Russia has never truly accepted Ukraine's independence.

The two countries have a long history: from the 9th to the 11th century, the State of Kiev, which covers present-day Ukraine, was the first state of the Eastern Slavs, before the Grand Duchy of Muscovy, which later became Russia, was established. Mainly part of the Russian Empire in the 17th and 18th centuries, Ukraine was independent only from 1918 to 1920, before returning to the USSR. The collapse of the Soviet bloc enabled Ukraine to break away from its imposing neighbor and become independent in 1991. But the influence of the new Russian state is still very much present in the country, with a strong presence of Russian minorities, and in Ukrainian political life. 2005 was a crucial year: Ukrainians voted in favor of pro-Russian Viktor Yanukovych in the presidential election. The result provoked a series of demonstrations, known as the "Orange Revolution", which led to the cancellation of the election and, ultimately, the election of President Viktor Yushchenko. This situation does not displease Russia, since the new Ukrainian president wishes to detach himself from Moscow's influence in order to obtain eventual membership of the European Union and NATO.

In 2010, Yanukovych regained power through the ballot box and began a rapprochement with his Russian ally, which explains his government's refusal to sign rapprochement agreements with the European Union in 2013. A crisis then erupted, leading to the Ukrainian Maidan revolution in 2014, followed by a change of governance and direction at the head of the country. Tensions soon

20. AFP dispatch, "UEFA: no matches between Russian and Ukrainian clubs", July 17, 2014.

flared between the predominantly Russian-speaking territories in the south-east of the country and the new central government in Kiev. Civil war broke out between pro-Russian separatists and the Ukrainian army in the Donbass region in the east of the country. Russia takes advantage of Ukraine's instability to exploit Crimea and annex the territory. On March 11, 2014, Crimea, where much of the Russian fleet resides in Sevastopol, proclaimed its independence. Then, following a referendum, Crimea became part of Russia on March 18, 2014. These events are condemned by Ukraine and a large part of the international community. Thus, on March 27, 2014, the UN General Assembly passed resolution 68/262 on "the territorial integrity of Ukraine", with the majority of countries contesting Crimea's attachment to Russia.

Relations between Russia and Ukraine will therefore be marked by this annexation, as well as continuing conflict in Ukraine's Donbass region, where pro-Russian militias are attempting to secede from the rest of the country. The situation intensified with Russia's military attack on Ukraine on February 24, 2022, sending shockwaves around the world, including in the sporting arena. In response to this invasion, political, economic and sporting sanctions were swiftly put in place to isolate and punish Russia, and above all to avoid a military escalation that could have led to fears of a wider world war. On February 28, 2022, the International Olympic Committee (IOC) recommended the exclusion of Russian and Belarusian athletes and teams from international competitions, a powerful decision by one of the world's most influential sports organizations. FIFA followed this recommendation by excluding Russia from the 2022 World Cup in Qatar, and UEFA withdrew Russian clubs from its competitions and the Russian national team from the Euro 2024 qualifiers.

These sanctions are not insignificant, since Russia, under the leadership of Vladimir Putin since 2000, had made sport a weapon of soft power, seeking to restore its image and demonstrate its return as a great power on the international stage after the fall of the USSR. For geopolitical doctor Lukas Aubin, Putin has put in place "a political-economic-sports system [sportokratura], which uses oligarchs, politicians and sportsmen and women to build an ultra-efficient sports model."[21] This strategy went even further in the early 2010s, with the organization of major sporting competitions to demonstrate Russia's return to the forefront, including the Sochi Winter Olympics in 2014 and the Football World Cup in 2018. However, Russia's "sport power" strategy was slowed by revelations around Russian state doping from 2015, leading to a "suspension" from international competitions, before being aggravated by the 2022 sanctions linked to the war in Ukraine.

Faced with these exclusions, the Russian Football Union (RFS) attempted to appeal the FIFA and UEFA decisions to the Court of Arbitration for Sport, but without success. In an effort to reintegrate into the sporting world, Russia is exploring other avenues, including integration into Asian sports federations. A friendly match between Russia and Iran in March 2023, followed by the Russian team's participation in the Central Asian Football Association championship, demonstrates this attempt to circumvent sporting isolation. In the end, Russian leaders voted unanimously against the option of joining the Asian Football Association on December 20, 2023. RFU member Mikhail Gerchkovich justifies this decision by stressing that "we have decided to continue contacts with UEFA, especially

21. Aubin Lukas, *La sportokratura sous Vladimir Poutine*, éditions Bréal, 2021.

as there is progress", reflecting cautious optimism about repairing relations with European soccer's governing body.

It's true that in October 2023, FIFA and UEFA attempted to reinstate Russian U-17 teams in competitions. However, this attempt was perceived by Ukraine and other countries (such as England, Poland and Sweden) as rehabilitating Russia and in a way endorsing the war launched by Vladimir Putin. This led the soccer authorities to abandon the plan. However, the tide is turning at the highest level of world sport, with the IOC authorizing Russian and Belarusian athletes to take part in the Paris 2024 Olympic Games in 2023. The Olympic movement is thus keen to return to a "neutral" position with regard to athletes who are nationals of a country, while maintaining a firm stance on their participation and not giving too many pledges to Russia and its precedents of sporting instrumentalization. Thus, athletes will only be able to take part in the Olympic Games as individuals, under a neutral banner, without any direct link to or support for the war in Ukraine, and in compliance with anti-doping regulations. While several Russian-influenced international sports federations, such as fencing, have begun to reintegrate Russian athletes, organizations such as FIFA and UEFA have yet to budge on their positions, since a national team can be such a symbolic and tense force.

Such is the case with the Ukrainian national team. Its qualification for Euro 2024 is more than just sporting. Already at Euro 2021, where Ukraine and Russia were present, the Ukrainian national team wore a jersey featuring their entire territory, including the outline of Crimea on the jersey, a territory annexed by Russia in 2014, arousing the ire of Moscow at the time. The jersey also featured the words "Glory to Ukraine! Glory to the Heroes!", the emblematic slogan of the popular Maïdan uprising in 2014. In response to the controversy surrounding these outfits, UEFA responded by stating that the map included on the shirts, integrating Crimea into Ukrainian territory, posed no problem from the organization's point of view, as it corresponded to the borders recognized by the United Nations. However, UEFA took a firm stance on the slogans on the shirts, ordering their removal. The European soccer authority justified its decision by pointing out that "the specific combination of these two slogans is considered to be clearly political in nature, possessing historical and militaristic significance".

Ukraine's participation in Euro 2024 will in any case be highly political, and is above all already a victory for an entire people, showing that the Ukrainian nation is still there, even though its territorial integrity and very existence are under threat. The reaction of Volodymyr Zelensky, President of Ukraine, testifies to the strength of this qualification: "Thanks guys! Thanks to the team! For the great emotions offered to the whole country. Thank you for demonstrating once again that every time Ukrainians face difficulties but don't give up and continue the fight, Ukrainians win. At a time when the enemy is trying to destroy us, we prove every day that Ukrainians are and will remain. Ukraine is and will remain! Glory to Ukraine!

Ukraine's qualification for Euro 2024 is much more than a sporting achievement but an act of resistance in the war it is waging against Russia, and the sporting representations of their national teams will remain a political marker for a long time to come.

8. The Case of Kosovo

Independent since 2008, Kosovo's existence as a sovereign state continues to be called into question. It has to be said that this Balkan territory has a complex history with its neighbor, Serbia, which is doing everything in its power with its allies to ensure that it is not recognized internationally. While its entry into the UN may be blocked, Kosovo is not short of resources. The Kosovar state does not hesitate to use its national soccer team to try and break down the political barriers of this diplomatic imbroglio.

Open warfare is not the only event that prevents two national teams from playing each other. Political tensions between two countries, which may have experienced conflicts, prevent other matches at European soccer level. This is the case for the Kosovo national team, which cannot play against Serbia and Bosnia-Herzegovina in an official match. It has to be said that the Kosovar question raises a lot of tension with its Balkan neighbors. Why should this be? The existence of this former Yugoslavian state has been disputed since its declaration of independence in 2008. Recognized by FIFA and UEFA, but not by the UN, Kosovo uses soccer as a diplomatic channel to assert its existence and re-enter the game of nations.

What is Kosovo? It's a Central European territory of around 10,000 km2 (the size of the Gironde département), landlocked between Albania, Northern Macedonia, Montenegro and Serbia. Kosovo's history is a complex one, intimately linked to that of its Albanian and Serbian neighbors. In 1878, at the Berlin Congress of Nations, the Kingdom of Serbia became independent and was granted the territory of present-day Kosovo. In the Serbian imagination, this land is associated with the battle of Kosovo Polje on June 15, 1389, or the battle of the "Field of Blackbirds", which saw the Ottoman Empire clash with a coalition of Christian princes, notably from Serbia. This battle founded the myth that Kosovo was the cradle of the Serbian nation.

Later, during the Second World War, Kosovo became part of Albania, then under the control of Fascist Italy. After the war and the creation of the Eastern bloc under the aegis of the USSR, Tito, the Yugoslav Communist leader, intended to create a federation of the various Balkan countries, the Socialist Federal Republic of Yugoslavia. This antagonized USSR leader Stalin, who wanted to control all the countries of Eastern Europe. In 1948, the break between the Soviet and Yugoslav states was complete. Relations were severed. Albania joined the great cohort of "people's democracies", while Kosovo was integrated into Yugoslavia as an autonomous province.

However, after the death of the authoritarian Tito in 1980, the first nationalist demonstrations broke out in this large federation. Kosovo, with its majority Albanian population, wanted to become a republic in its own right. Yugoslavia's Communist rulers, influenced by the Republic of Serbia and its leader Slobodan Milošević, disagreed and harshly repressed the riots. With the collapse of the USSR, from 1989 onwards, many Eastern Bloc nations fought for their independence, causing a snowball effect within the Yugoslav Federal Republic: several of its members demanded independence. This was the case for Slovenia, Croatia and Bosnia. Slobodan Milošević's Serbia tried by force to save what remained of the federation, triggering the bloody Yugoslav wars. The Dayton Accords of 1995 put an end to this inter-ethnic fighting and to the great federation of Yugoslavia, which was now composed of Serbia, Montenegro and Kosovo.

However, the new republic was not finished with the war, as independence aspirations began to emerge in the south. In 1998, a new war broke out in Kosovo between Albanian separatists and Serbian forces, resulting in over 13,000 deaths and mass emigration. NATO intervention in 1999 put an end to the armed conflict and to the repressive, violent regime of Slobodan Milošević.

Kosovo remained a territory with undetermined status until 2007. In fact, it was not until this date that former Finnish President Martti Ahtisaari, who was overseeing negotiations between the Serbian and Kosovar governments, submitted a proposal to the United Nations Security Council to grant Kosovo the status of an independent state. Russia, a permanent member of the Council, vetoed the resolution on the grounds that independence would be contrary to the principle of territorial unity of its Serbian ally. Kosovo's provisional parliament, however, did not wait for UN approval and unilaterally declared independence on February 17, 2008.

Since then, a long diplomatic battle has been waged to have Kosovo recognized as such. By September 4, 2020, (approximately) 98 of the 193 members of the United Nations had recognized Kosovo's independence, including the United States, France and

Germany. Although present in several international organizations (IMF, World Bank), the new Kosovar state is not part of one of the most important, the UN, due to the Russian veto. Russia and Serbia are not the only countries fiercely opposed to recognizing Kosovo as a state. This is also the case for China and Spain, for whom recognition of this independence would send a positive signal to the supporters of strong regionalist claims within their borders (Tibet and Xinjiang in China, Basque Country and Catalonia in Spain). As for Serbia, it has been waging a major diplomatic campaign since 2017 to get certain states to restrict visas for Kosovar nationals and revoke their decision to recognize Kosovo. Since March 2, 2020, and Sierra Leone's revocation, 15 countries have taken this route.

In addition to this diplomatic conflict, a territorial dispute persists between Serbia and Kosovo. The Serb-majority north of Kosovo does not recognize the authority of Pristina, the capital of Kosovo, but that of Belgrade. This can lead to dramatic situations, as when, at the end of 2018, the Kosovar government introduced a tax on all products imported from Serbia and Bosnia-Herzegovina, countries with a large Serbian minority. This tax had a major impact on the Serbian population in northern Kosovo. To avoid a humanitarian catastrophe in July 2019, Pristina is sending foodstuffs there, but local Serbs are refusing to buy them, fearing they will be poisoned by Albanians.

These diplomatic and territorial tensions explain why a match between Kosovo and Serbia or Kosovo and Bosnia-Herzegovina, under the aegis of UEFA, cannot take place. For fear that a battle on the pitch could lead to conflict. The memory of the famous match between Dinamo Zagreb and Red Star Belgrade at the Maksimir stadium on May 13, 1990, will live long in the memory. For the press at the time, it was the kick-off to the Yugoslav wars. Although the reality is more complex (see chapter 4), the outbursts at this match transcended national borders and highlighted the eminently political role of soccer in the Balkans.

Football played a major role in Kosovar resistance in the 1990s, as explained in detail in Loïc Trégourès' book *Le Football dans le chaos Ygoslave*[22]. It was a means of resisting Serbia, structuring Kosovar civil society and fighting for independence. It has continued to be used since 2008, as Kosovo uses sport to exist on the international stage. Sporting representation enables the Kosovan nation to showcase its colors and flag. Kosovo, for example, has been a member of the International Olympic Committee (IOC) since 2014, giving it the opportunity to send a delegation of athletes to the 2016 Rio Olympics. On this occasion, judoka Majlinda Kelmendi won Olympic gold and allowed the Kosovar anthem, "Europe", to be played before billions of television viewers following the competition.

As far as soccer is concerned, it's a longer road to reach the queen of competitions, the World Cup. It has already been a battle to become a member of UEFA and FIFA. This was achieved on May 3, 2016, when 28 of the 54 members of the UEFA Congress voted in favor of Kosovo's membership. FIFA membership followed, enabling the *Dardanians*, as the Kosovo team is known, to take part in both the World Cup and Euro qualifiers. An essential recognition, given that soccer is such an important part of the Kosovan nation, and a feat made possible thanks to former player Fadil Vokrri, President of the Kosovo Football Federation, who sadly passed away in 2018[23].

22. TRÉGOURÈS Loïc, *op. cit.*—chap. 10, p. 175.
23. LEFEVRE Florian, "Fadil Vokrri", *So Foot*, June 2020.

With just 2 million inhabitants, Kosovo is far from ridiculous on the footballing planet, as the national team has strung together an impressive run of 15 games without defeat between March 24, 2018 and September 10, 2019. It has risen from 190th in the FIFA rankings in 2016 to 102nd today. If the team is progressing so quickly, and is no longer a "small selection", it is largely because it relies on its strong diaspora, i.e. the dispersal of its community after the war and still today across Europe. There are, for example, some 200,000 Kosovars in Switzerland, representing 10% of Kosovo's current population. The national team is therefore largely made up of players who were not born in the country, or who have already played at international level under other colors.

Above all, players of Albanian origin, and therefore close to the Kosovar identity, mobilized long before 2016 to ensure that this team existed on the pitch. In 2012, Albanian international Lorik Cana, along with Swiss players Granit Xhaka, Valon Behrami and Xherdan Shaqiri, all of Kosovar Albanian origin, wrote to FIFA to request that Kosovo be allowed to play official friendly matches, an initiative supported by many other footballers. In 2016, FIFA authorized the players to play for the *Dardanians*, after having worn the jersey of another national team.

This has not been the case for Switzerland's Shaqiri and Xhaka since the new FIFA regulations came into force. However, the two friends are very attached to Kosovo. In fact, during Switzerland's victory over Serbia at the 2018 World Cup, they celebrated their team's goals by linking their hands with their thumbs. A gesture that is by no means insignificant, since it symbolizes the two-headed eagle, the Albanian rallying sign. FIFA then fined the players, prompting the Kosovar and Albanian sides to open an online kitty. Kosovo's then Minister of Trade and Industry also contributed, donating 1,500 euros—his entire salary. For Kosovo's current coach, the Swiss Bernard Challandes, convincing players to come and play for the blue and yellow team is becoming less and less complicated, as there's now a dynamic around the national team. Such enthusiasm could have enabled Kosovo to take part in Euro 2021, but a defeat by neighboring Northern Macedonia postponed this objective.

Despite its disputed status, and impossible matches against Serbia and Bosnia-Herzegovina, soccer remains the best tool for recognition and hope for a relatively poor territory subject to high emigration. It's not for nothing that the Kosovar government set up a ministry for the diaspora in 2011. Participation in an international soccer competition would highlight the situation of Kosovo, which, like Serbia, is keen to join the European Union for a better future.

Of course, the issue remains unresolved, since some EU members do not officially recognize Kosovo. This is the case of Spain, which recently caused a stir when its soccer federation questioned the territory's existence. On the occasion of a World Cup 2022 qualifying match on March 31, the Spanish Football Federation announced that its national team was playing against "the territory of Kosovo" and that the team could not display the symbols of the Kosovar nation. Kosovo was quick to challenge this decision, threatening not to play the match. Doubtless for fear of being excluded by FIFA, Spain backed down and the match finally went ahead normally. Proof that Kosovo still has a long way to go, and that soccer plays an eminently political role in its recognition.

9. Gibraltar-Spain

In the south of Spain, Gibraltar, a "rock" of around 6 km2, is the subject of one of the oldest diplomatic conflicts, between Spain and the United Kingdom. A conflict that has taken another turn since 2013, when Gibraltar won its battle with its Spanish neighbor to be able to take part in official soccer matches thanks to its national team. Madrid is not about to accept the situation, and is still trying to establish its sovereignty over the territory.

As we mentioned in the previous chapter, Spain remains opposed to the recognition of Kosovo. This is not the only geo-politico-football situation on which Madrid remains deadlocked. There's another, which concerns a smaller territory, a "rock". We're not talking about Monaco here, but about an enclave that generates a lot of tension: Gibraltar. Indeed, this land has the distinction of being a small British overseas territory (6.8 km2) that shares a border of barely one kilometer with its Spanish neighbor. A strategic piece of land nonetheless, since it gives its name to the famous Strait of Gibraltar, the maritime gateway between the Atlantic Ocean and the Mediterranean Sea.

Why is a British territory so far from its metropolis? To understand this, we need to look back in history. Until then a Spanish territory, Gibraltar came under the British flag in 1713, following the War of Spanish Succession and the Treaty of Utrecht. Since then, this "rock" has been repeatedly claimed by Spain, particularly in the 1960s. With the advent of decolonization, the Spanish government attempted to reclaim it by raising the issue at the United Nations, under the pretext of putting an end to Gibraltar's "colonial" situation, in accordance with the principle of "the right of peoples to self-determination". Faced with this diplomatic offensive, the United Kingdom counter-attacked and submitted a referendum to the Gibraltarians in 1967. The result was indisputable: 99.64% of Gibraltarians expressed their wish to remain under British sovereignty. As a result, Spanish dictator Franco closed the border between Spain and Gibraltar. This was not re-established until 1985.

The main point of disagreement concerns control of territorial waters and fishing zones, since the British crown has de facto access to Gibraltar's advantageous location. This is why Spain wants to abrogate the agreements, which date back to the 18th century. The context tends to change, as Madrid no longer seeks to recover the territory, but rather to set up a Spanish-British co-sovereignty (similar to what is done for Andorra with France). In 2016, Spain reformulated its proposal to share sovereignty, but the Gibraltarians, who had already rejected the idea in a referendum in November 2002, maintained their position. The relative autonomy of this British territory is regularly called into question by its imposing neighbor. For this reason, Gibraltar has been looking for ways to emphasize its special status vis-à-vis the European Union and the United Kingdom for several years now.

One of these means is sport, and not just any sport, since the most popular sport among Gibraltar's 30,000 inhabitants is soccer. Its history goes back a long way, since the round ball was introduced to Gibraltar by the British military in the 19th century, and the first club, Prince of Wales FC, was founded in 1892. Soccer then developed with the appearance of numerous teams, culminating in the establishment of a championship. The Gibraltar national team was formed in 1923, in a match against Seville. However, this team only competed against local clubs, not national teams. It wasn't until the 1993 Island Games that Gibraltar played its first international match against the (also British) island of Jersey.

While the 1990s saw the emergence of new "small" national teams, such as San Marino, in the qualifiers for the World Cup or the Euro, Gibraltar applied for UEFA membership in 1999. The move was far from far-fetched, since teams such as the Faroe Islands, an autonomous territory of the Kingdom of Denmark, are members of this institution and play official international matches with their national teams. However, the case of Gibraltar is different, as Denmark was not opposed to this request. However, in the case of Gibraltar, although the United Kingdom has agreed to see its territory play under its own colors, this is seen as an affront by Spain, which still hopes to reclaim this piece of land. Moreover, the Spanish territory is subject to strong regionalist demands, and Madrid takes a dim view of a precedent likely to inspire the Basque Country or Catalonia, which have already set up unofficial national teams.

After being repeatedly refused membership of UEFA, Gibraltar reapplied in 2007, this time with the support of three major associations (England, Scotland and Wales). Spain did not say its last word, however, and put pressure on UEFA to restrict the membership rules for soccer federations to sovereign states recognized by the United

Nations. This is not the case for Gibraltar, a British overseas territory. This change in rules was contested by the Gibraltarian side, and the case was brought before the Court of Arbitration for Sport (CAS). Finally, in 2011, CAS ruled that Gibraltar's membership could not be refused because the new UEFA rules had only been established after the initial applications in 1999 and 2007. Subsequently, the Gibraltar Football Association was officially accepted as a full UEFA member on May 24, 2013, with only the Spanish and Belarusian federations objecting[24]. For the time being, therefore, UEFA does not authorize any matches between the Gibraltar and Spanish national teams. Gibraltar's first official international match took place on November 19, 2013, against Slovakia.

Gibraltar continued its quest to exist through sport by becoming a member of FIFA in 2016. Its beginnings were laborious, however, as, like many small teams, the Gibraltar team finished last in the various qualifying groups, failing to win any of the qualifiers for the Euros 2016 and 2020 and the 2018 World Cup. However, the situation is changing, thanks in particular to the Nations League, UEFA's new competition that allows teams of "similar level" to compete against each other and, why not? earn an unhoped-for ticket to take part in the Euro. The selection is making good progress thanks to this competition, as Gibraltar won its first two matches in official competition, against Armenia (1-0) and Liechtenstein (2-1). These victories over national teams accustomed to international encounters were enough to put the spotlight on an entire territory.

Although Gibraltar's national team is often defeated, its existence is of interest elsewhere, especially in view of the Brexit. This

24. Montague James, "Gibraltar moves closer to soccer independence", *New York Times*, May 2013.

national team legitimizes Gibraltar a little more, with the distribution of its flag, or the image of its atypical stadium on the side of a rock, Victoria Stadium. Important elements for this territory of the United Kingdom whose future is uncertain. In the 2016 Brexit referendum, nearly 95.6% of Gibraltarians voted for the UK to remain a member of the European Union. It has to be said that every day, almost 14,000 people cross the border from Campo de Gibraltar, a neighboring Spanish territory where unemployment is approaching 40%. With Brexit, the entire economy of the Rock is at risk. Faced with this risk, Gibraltar's head of government, Fabian Picardo, wants to join the Schengen area, of which the UK is not a member, to preserve this freedom of movement. In particular, Gibraltar wants to follow the example of other European microstates, such as Liechtenstein, an associate member of the Schengen area. Spain and the UK have already held discussions in 2018 on Gibraltar's situation, signing bilateral agreements on citizens' rights and administrative, police and customs cooperation.

On January 31, 2020, the UK and Gibraltar effectively left the European Union. However, in December 2020, the UK and Spanish governments agreed in principle that the UK and EU could negotiate the terms of Gibraltar's participation in certain aspects of the Schengen Agreement, negotiations still ongoing in 2024. Spain, however, remains on the lookout to reiterate its co-sovereignty project and grant dual passports to Gibraltar's inhabitants, who would thus regain freedom of movement. This would also enable Madrid to win a diplomatic battle that has been going on for centuries. However, it will be difficult to question the territory's existence, given that its national soccer team has taken on the role of ambassador for this small but strategic territory.

10. Armenia-Azerbaijan

The Azerbaijani military offensive in Nagorno-Karabakh in September 2023 has once again highlighted the tensions between Armenia and Azerbaijan. While the virtues of sport are often put forward to ease diplomatic relations, the situation between the two states is such that no international matches are possible between their national soccer teams. This is due to the geopolitical situation in Nagorno-Karabakh, a region that both sides claim as their own because of its historical past. No referee is about to blow the whistle on this game between two irreconcilable countries.

Matches between Armenia and Azerbaijan are also "impossible" under UEFA rules. A meeting between these two countries may at first glance be puzzling, as they are not clearly defined as being part of Europe. They are in fact part of Western Asia and the Caucasus region, although the latter has had a history intimately linked to the European and Asian continents. Both states are, for example, members of the Council of Europe, an intergovernmental organization for the defense of human rights and the development of democratic stability in Europe. The soccer federations of these two countries joined UEFA (in 1993 and 1994) rather than the Asian Football Confederation, just a few years after their independence.

Armenia and Azerbaijan are, in fact, "young" independent states, having gained their independence from the Soviet republics in the early 1990s. However, both countries have had a tumultuous history since the beginning of the 20th century. After the First World War and the dissolution of the Transcaucasian Federation, Azerbaijan and Armenia first proclaimed their independence on the same day, May 28, 1918. War broke out very quickly afterwards, as both entities laid claim to territories they considered historically and ethnically theirs. They were eventually annexed by the USSR, which put an end to the conflict for a time. Soviet leader Stalin unilaterally decided that the Nagorno-Karabakh region, populated mainly by Christian Armenians, should revert to Azerbaijan, with its Muslim majority. It was only when the Soviet empire disintegrated at the end of the 1980s that nationalist tendencies resurfaced in both countries, particularly in the Nagorno-Karabakh region.

In 1988, the local population revolted and the region declared itself a republic in its own right. This led to a series of acts of violence in the territory, which quickly descended into war. The conflict continued after the dissolution of the USSR in 1991. While Armenia and Azerbaijan declared their independence, Nagorno-Karabakh did likewise, so as not to become part of Azerbaijan. As a result, Azerbaijan set up a blockade on the region and its main Armenian ally. After hundreds of deaths and injuries, the conflict was finally frozen in 1994, thanks to a ceasefire. The Minsk Group, co-chaired by France, Russia and the United States, negotiated a final resolution to the conflict, but no lasting solution was found.

The question of Nagorno-Karabakh is still far from resolved. The region even descended into war again in 2016, when Azerbaijan launched an offensive to reclaim the territory, triggering the Four-Day War. Nagorno-Karabakh, for its part, amended its constitution by referendum in 2017, taking the name of Republic of Artsakh, in reference to the tenth province of the Kingdom of Armenia, thus reaffirming its desire not to be under Azeri control. The war resurfaced on September 27, 2020, when the city of Stepanakert was bombed, triggering a cascade of diplomatic incidents and the mobilization of Armenian and Azerbaijani armed forces. The war ends on November 10, 2020, when a trilateral ceasefire agreement is signed between Azerbaijan, Armenia and Russia. The balance of power shifted in September 2023 when Azerbaijan launched a military offensive on the territory of Nagorno-Karabakh, resulting in a ceasefire and the laying down of arms by the separatists: Nagorno-Karabakh became de facto part of Azerbaijan.

The history of conflicts has therefore forced UEFA to continue its ban on any international confrontation between the national soccer teams of these two countries. There has been one attempt in the past, during Euro 2008 qualifying. As luck would have it, Armenia and Azerbaijan were drawn in the same group. Unfortunately, the matches never took place, as the two countries were unable to reach a compromise. The matches were simply cancelled, and both teams finished bottom of the group. Proof that sport is far from apolitical, and that it cannot solve all ills. Recent history bears witness to this when, for example, Armenian player Henrikh Mkhitaryan refused to attend the 2019 Europa League final because it was being held in Baku, the capital of Azerbaijan. The player and the Armenian Football Federation also react in September 2020, the period of the conflict in Nagorno-Karabakh, when an executive of Azeri club Qarabağ FK is accused of publishing a message of hatred towards Armenia and defending the Armenian genocide of 1915. Despite calls for the club to be excluded from European competitions, nothing has been done.

Qarabağ FK is a typical example of Armenian-Azerbaijani tensions. The club was founded in 1951 in the town of Agdam, located in Nagorno-Karabakh. The town was taken over in 1993 by the armed forces of the new regional republic, leading to the exodus of its Azeri inhabitants and the club's move to the capital, Baku. However, since its takeover in 2001 by one of Azerbaijan's largest companies, Azersun Holding, Qarabağ FK has established itself as the country's leading club. This is far from insignificant, since, unlike Armenian clubs, Qarabağ FK is starting to become a regular in European competitions. In fact, it was the first Azeri club to qualify for the Champions League group stage in 2017. Thanks to this exposure, Azerbaijan is now better placed on the map by millions of television viewers. This sporting success bears the hallmark of the team's coach, Gurban Gurbanov, who wants to make it a sporting reference, "the Barcelona of the Caucasus", and a showcase for the Azeri cause demanding their return to Nagorno-Karabakh. Soccer is also a vehicle for supporters of independence for the "Republic of Artsakh". The region's national team has taken part in a number of unofficial international matches since 2012, even organizing a CONIFA European Cup in 2019 in Nagorno-Karabakh, which we'll discuss in more detail in a few chapters.

Soccer is more than just a sport in Azerbaijan. In recent years, Azerbaijan has been investing to become a new sporting stronghold. European Games in 2015, Formula 1 Grand Prix since 2016, Europa League final 2019 and, this summer, Euro 2021 matches in Baku. Azerbaijan is following in the footsteps of many other states, which are using the organization of sporting events to attract international attention and boost the image of this country with its authoritarian regime. In the words of the country's Minister of Sport, Azad Rahimov, for whom "[each] of these events strengthens Azerbaijan's place on the world map and creates the conditions for increasing tourism"[25], and who boasts of the "83 million television viewers who watched the Baku Formula 1 Grand Prix in 2018" This was also the case during Euro 2021, when the capital Baku hosted several matches, highlighting a country that has been investing in soccer for many years. As witnessed by Socar, the national oil company, a major UEFA sponsor since 2013, which bought Atletico de Madrid's sponsorship at a high price so that the country's tourism slogan (*Land of fire*) could be displayed on the club's jersey from 2013 to 2015.

However, the desire to exist through sport and to improve one's image through major international sporting events can have a downside. If Azerbaijan is in the spotlight, so too is the authoritarian regime of Ilham Aliyev, President of Azerbaijan since 2003, and its bellicose policy towards Armenia. Following Azerbaijan's military victory in Nagorno-Karabakh in September 2023, Armenia played the diplomatic card by proposing a non-aggression pact to its neighbor. At the beginning of 2024, however, this proposal failed to materialize, with renewed military tensions along the border following the re-election of President Aliev, who has been in power for two decades in this hydrocarbon-rich country. Armenia and Azerbaijan remain back to back, and no amount of soccer will accelerate the peace process.

---

25. Dépêche AFP, "Ligue Europa: à Bakou, le sport en vitrine du régime", May 2019.

III. Atypical Teams and Competitions

11. Soccer's Other Europe: CONIFA

While the Euro soccer tournament is taking place this summer, an atypical competition is bringing together countries and regions that are not officially independent: the European Cup of the Confederation of Independent Football Associations (CONIFA). This competition has the particularity of highlighting soccer teams representing certain minorities, ethnic groups and contested regions, which exist thanks to soccer.

The Euro is not the only competition to bring together international teams for a European soccer competition. There is also the Confederation of Independent Football Associations (CONIFA), an organization that brings together teams from states not recognized at international level, such as those from minorities and disputed regions. These teams are not eligible to join the official world soccer organization, FIFA, partly because of a lack of infrastructure, and partly because such "national teams" lead to diplomatic difficulties with certain states. This is the challenge facing CONIFA, which aims to shed light on populations with complex geopolitical situations. This confederation came into being on June 7, 2013, following the demise of NF-Board, which had been organizing competitions between such teams since 2006. According to its articles of association, its aim is to "contribute to the strengthening of global relations and build bridges between people, nations, minorities and isolated regions around the world through friendship, culture and the joy of playing soccer"[26].

This organization is taking up the torch in fine style, organizing several international competitions, the first of which was a World Cup held in Lapland in 2014 (more on this in the next chapter). Numerous teams took part, including one from Kurdistan—the Kurds form a population with no real state, living mainly in Turkey, Iran, Iraq and Syria—or Abkhazia, a territory that proclaimed its independence from Georgia in 1992, but whose situation is currently recognized by only a small number of states, including Russia. Of the 12 teams taking part, Comté de Nice, a selection of players set up to promote the culture and identity of Nice, won the trophy against the Isle of Man. For Franck Delerue, a player from the Comté de Nice, "it was an incredible experience, we changed countries, discovered new cultures, regions of the world we knew absolutely nothing about"[27].

Since then, two other editions of this World Cup have taken place. In 2016 in Abkhazia and in 2018 in London, where the host team was Barawa, a Somali diaspora based in the UK. It was on this occasion that the CONIFA competition brought together the largest number of teams, 16 in all, from Tibet to the Tuvalu Islands and Kabylie. Nearly 3,000 spectators from all walks of life gathered in the

---

26. CONIFA website.

27. Menetier Denis, "Comté de Nice, Ruthénie subcarpatique, Abkhazie... bienvenue à la CONIFA, l'antichambre de la FIFA", *France TV Sport*, February 2021.

Enfield stadium. The strong Cypriot community in the British capital also rallied to support the finalist team, from the Turkish Republic of Northern Cyprus, which, as its name suggests, is a territory in the north-east of the island of Cyprus, recognized only by Turkey. In the end, it was the team from Subcarpathian Ruthenia (to which I'll return later) that won this edition. Organizing such competitions is no easy task, however, since unlike the influential FIFA, only the players' stay is insured. This means that travel expenses, staff and so on are covered by the team. This complicates travel for teams from America, Asia and Africa, as CONIFA tournaments are mainly held in Europe, and forces many to forego participation for lack of funds.

In addition to material constraints, there are other issues to consider. Notably the diplomatic dimension, since some countries do not want their territorial integrity to be contested, as in the case of China, which protested against the presence of the Tibetan team at the CONIFA 2018 World Cup, or Ukraine, in reaction to the victory of Subcarpathian Ruthenia, a region of Ukraine with a large Hungarian minority, at the same World Cup. The Ukrainian authorities denounced this as "sporting separatism", with the result that the players selected were banned from playing at professional and amateur level in Ukraine.

Other selections have different claims, such as Cascadia. This team represents the bio-region of the same name, in the north-west of the American continent. At the same World Cup, when journalist Matthew Engel asked the question, "Who oppresses the Cascadians?", one of the team's players replied, "Anyone who harms the planet."[28]

---

28. DUEZ Julien, "We were at the CONIFA World Cup final", *So Foot*, June 2018.

In any case, diplomatic problems remain the main obstacle to the development of these selections, as shown by the example of the latest CONIFA European Cup 2019 in a highly sensitive region, Nagorno-Karabakh or the Republic of Artsakh. The competition is a way for the region to showcase its status as a self-proclaimed republic to Azerbaijan, which claims sovereignty over the territory. This has led to pressure from the Azeri side for certain teams not to take part—as in the case of the teams from Sardinia and the Donetsk People's Republic. The European Cup nevertheless went ahead, with South Ossetia winning the final against Western Armenia.

However, CONIFA President Per-Anders Blind denies any politicization of events: "We don't play politics. Soccer is in my blood and politics is of little importance to me. Our members are often people who have been historically brutalized and who have low self-esteem. CONIFA's aim is simply to give them the opportunity to show off their beauty, and to educate the world by putting them on the map."[29] Brutalized populations in the image of the Chagos Islands, representing an Indian Ocean people expelled from their islands over 50 years ago by the United Kingdom to make an American military base on the main island of Diego Garcia.

In 2020, the World Cup was due to take place in Northern Macedonia, but the Covid-19 epidemic has postponed the competition to a later date. For all that, CONIFA's future is clouded. The organization is beginning to experience the same power struggles as its big sister, FIFA. Paul Watson, former organizer of the 2018 World Cup, points to the fact that certain European federations are privileged over others, particularly in view of their economic base.

---

29. Menetier Denis, "Comté de Nice, Ruthénie subcarpatique, Abkhazie... bienvenue à la CONIFA, l'antichambre de la FIFA", *France TV Sport*, February 2021.

In other words, if the federations, most of which are voluntary, don't pay their dues, they can't take part in CONIFA competitions.

Although the Covid-19 epidemic has considerably slowed down the project of these World Cups of non-existent countries, care must be taken to ensure that these fine initiatives, centered around ignored peoples or minorities, do not turn into a place where favoritism reigns. The "resistance" is getting organized, as some CONIFA members have created the World Unity Football Alliance, a group of federations seeking to organize competitions for themselves, without any hierarchy or political game. Nor has CONIFA given up hope of organizing a major international competition again, with the announcement of a forthcoming World Cup in the summer of 2024 in Kurdistan, which will bring together no fewer than 16 teams from Kabylia to Tibet, via South Ossetia.

Be that as it may, these various selections once again demonstrate that soccer is more than just a sport, and that you can express yourself as much with your feet as with your words.

12. Lapland: the National Selection of Santa's lands

Proof of the global impact of soccer, even Santa Claus has got in on the act! Beyond this narrative facility, Lapland is indeed a territory made up of an ancient indigenous people, the Sami. Today, soccer remains one of the rare unifying elements of this people who stretch across four different countries.

Lapland. This name is not insignificant, as it is often associated with Santa's imaginary land of reindeer and elves. Yet this territory is very real. It stretches across the northern regions of four countries: Norway, Sweden, Finland and north-west Russia. Throughout its history, Lapland has been inhabited by the indigenous nomadic Sami people, who today number 100,000. This people should not be called "Lappish", as this term is pejorative in Swedish: it means "ragged". For this reason, the territory is not called Lapland in the local language, but Sápmi.

The term "discriminatory" comes as no surprise, given the history of persecution of this minority throughout the 20th century. The various Sami peoples living in Norway and Sweden had been trying to unite since 1917, when the first Sami congress was held in Trondheim, Norway. This was the first time that Norwegian and Swedish Sami had met outside their national borders to work together to find solutions to common problems. These different populations were finally assimilated. This was the case in Norway, where a policy aimed at "absorbing these people" and integrating them into the Norwegian nation was put in place, *with* laws restricting the Sami's right to buy land, practice their culture or even speak the Sami language, until 1959. The same was true of Sweden, where discrimination continued until 1970.

The situation for the locals subsequently improved, as their rights were gradually recognized. The Sámi have developed ways of promoting their culture. One of the ways they do this is through sport and football. On July 19, 1985, a team from the Far North played its first international match against Åland, an autonomous province of Finland. In the end, Lapland lost 4-2, but there was more to it than that. Above all, this match is historic. It was broadcast live on the radio in northern Norway and Sweden, shedding light on a people too long forgotten and persecuted. The players of the time still remember it, as Kalle Tjäder, the very first striker for the Lapland team, testifies: "It was wonderful. It was Lapland's first international match and we had to score. I really wasn't expecting it."[30]

This match was part of the Sámi social movement of the 1980s for greater recognition of their rights as an indigenous people. Progress led to the Nordic Sami Conference in Åre, Sweden, on August 15, 1986, which adopted the first Sami flag, featuring the colors red, green, yellow and blue, adorned with a circle representing the

30. Kejonen Olle, "1985: Sápmis första landskamp", *Sverige Radio*, August 2015.

sun and moon. Subsequently, the "Sami Parliaments" of Norway, Sweden and Finland were created to represent the claims of this minority to national governments. This is not the case on the Russian side, where no such representative body is recognized. The three parliaments often work together on cross-border issues, but there is no single, unified Sami parliament covering the Nordic countries. For the time being, they have very little political influence, a far cry from autonomy.

The Lapland team, meanwhile, continued its ascent, playing matches against genuine national teams such as the East German U-21 team in 1987, and Estonia in 1990. This rapid development prompted the Lapland Football Association to apply for FIFA membership in 2001, following in the footsteps of the Danish Faroe Islands. The procedure was unsuccessful, however, and the Lapland team continued its world tour. It has to be said that, since the 2000s, federations have been created so that teams not accepted as FIFA members can compete against each other.

In 2006, the Nordics struck a blow by winning the Viva World Cup 2006, one of the first international competitions of its kind for these selections[31]. The final victory was a resounding 21-1 over the Monaco national team! This is partly due to the fact that the Sami national team included several professional players from the Norwegian and Swedish leagues, including former Norwegian international Tom Høgli, who went on to become a true ambassador for the Sami identity.

This performance enables the Lapland team to showcase its culture and its fight for greater recognition. Above all, on paper,

31. DOWLING Tim, "The World Cup sides you've never heard of", *The Guardian*, June 2008.

this selection brings together all the Sami communities, whereas in the political arena the parliaments are not yet united. Because of this lack of unity, the question of autonomy for the region is not yet on the agenda. This selection's struggle is more focused on better consideration of the rights of the indigenous population. This lack of coordination is not helping the Lapland team to develop, and is preventing it from fulfilling the conditions for membership of the FIFA or UEFA soccer organizations. As a result, it is still unable to take part in official international matches or tournaments, such as the World Cup qualifiers. Nevertheless, the team's various tours play a major role in raising international awareness of the rights of the Sami people.

This dynamic slowed down in the early 2010s, with the Lapland Football Association experiencing significant financial problems, leading to the creation of a new structure in 2014, the FA Sápmi. The latter wasted no time in hosting the first-ever CONIFA World Cup in Östersund, Sweden, in 2014. The event brings together 12 teams, from Kurdistan to the Isle of Man and Nagorno-Karabakh. The team from Lapland doesn't win a single match, leaving the County of Nice to win the competition.

The Sámi subsequently take part in other international tournaments, another edition of the World Cup in 2016 in Abkhazia and the 2019 European Cup in Nagorno-Karabakh. Lapland failed to win any of these competitions. It is currently ranked 19th in the CONIFA world rankings, and the team has not won an international title since its 2006 trophy. It is no longer a major selection among non-FIFA teams. One of the reasons for the team's lacklustre results is the growing reluctance of professional clubs in Norway and Sweden to release their players of Sami origin, given their increasingly busy schedules. The interest lies elsewhere for this team. Above all, it's a way of highlighting the identity of the Sami nation, to which 85,000 people lay claim, through a collective, cross-border project, and of making Lapland and its history more visible to the world.

13. Åland: a Quasi-State on UEFA's Doorstep

In the heart of the Baltic Sea, the Åland archipelago represents a unique enclave of culture, history and autonomy, celebrating the centenary of its special status in 2021. Its history and close links with Sweden and Finland make it a veritable "state within a state" in Finnish administration. Åland now sees a potential future in international sporting institutions such as UEFA and FIFA, in the same way as the Faroe Islands and Gibraltar.

Although Åland represents only 0.005% of the Finnish population and is the smallest region in Finland, it has enjoyed the status of autonomous province since 1921. But why? First, let's put Åland in context. Stretching over 1,580 km2 with some 6,500 islands, 60 to 80 of which are inhabited, Åland lies between Finland and Sweden, with 90% of its 29,000 inhabitants concentrated on the main island, Fasta Åland. Its capital, Mariehamn, is home to almost a third of the population.

Although today Åland is partly part of Finland, its history is closely linked to that of Sweden, since the islands became part of the Swedish kingdom from the 13th century, more specifically within the Duchy of Finland. The small archipelago's position in the Baltic Sea made it a coveted site, as whoever controlled Åland had a stranglehold on the entire Gulf of Bothnia. From the 18th century onwards, Russia launched several offensives against Sweden in a bid to reclaim this strategic node. Eventually, the islands were ceded to the Russian Empire, along with the rest of Finland, in the 1809 Treaty of Fredrikshamn. Proof of the archipelago's importance, French and British troops landed there in 1854 to disable the Russian navy in the Baltic: it was the Åland War. The territory remains in Russian hands, however, on condition that it remains demilitarized.

The situation changed during the First World War. After the Russian Revolution of 1917, Finland took advantage of the situation to regain its sovereignty, proclaiming its independence and calling for the Åland Islands to be attached to their country. The problem was that the archipelago's largely Swedish-speaking inhabitants and the Swedish state did not agree. Swedish troops took advantage of the Finnish civil war to occupy the islands militarily. On March 6, 1918, a German-Swedish agreement was signed for the division of the islands. At the end of the war, Finland wanted to reclaim what was rightfully theirs, but the people of Åland disagreed. 96% of the local population signed a petition calling for secession from Finland and integration with Sweden.

In 1921, the League of Nations (League) awarded Åland to Finland, on condition that the Finnish state undertook to respect and guarantee Ålanders the use of their Swedish language, culture and local customs. The territory is also granted self-governing status, meaning that the provincial powers normally exercised by representatives of the Finnish central government are largely exercised by its own government. The first meeting of Åland's autonomous legislative assembly took place on June 9, 2022, a date now celebrated each year as the archipelago's national holiday. What best characterizes this unique combination of Swedish and Finnish influence is the autonomous province's flag. This flag, featuring a yellow Nordic cross on a blue background, with a red cross at its heart, symbolizes Åland's belonging to Finland while highlighting its close ties with Sweden. Over the years, this autonomy has translated into specific legislative and administrative rights, enabling Åland to pursue internal and external policies distinct from those of mainland Finland. In a way, a "state within a state". In 1994, for example, Åland held a separate referendum on its integration into the European Union, with 73% approval. The preservation of its language and traditions, and its autonomous government, embody a form of "associated free state" which, while enjoying a high degree of autonomy, remains deeply linked to Finland and open to the outside world.

The presence of its own capital, parliament, elections and national symbols such as an anthem reflect Åland's strong cultural and political identity. This autonomy is reinforced by distinct local institutions and educational or administrative practices, such as the unique license plate model, which underline Åland's difference from the rest of Finland and, by extension, the European Union. These characteristics make Åland a fascinating case of balance between national belonging and regional autonomy, offering a model of regional governance that could inspire other regions seeking autonomy within their respective countries.

Another element by which Åland distinguishes itself, and which today is a not inconsiderable part of a country's national representation, is its national soccer team. The team was created in 1985, with a first match and a first victory against a team we've already mentioned, Lapland. Several friendly matches followed, before Åland took part in its first competition in the "Island Games" soccer tournament. These island "Olympic Games", created in 1985, are above all a means for island communities, whether autonomous or not, to promote their culture and heritage, while enabling athletes to compete at an international level. Above all, its national team enables Åland to brandish its national symbols (flag, anthem) at matches and sporting competitions, thus reinforcing the archipelago's special status and reaffirming a sense of belonging.

It's mainly thanks to these local clubs that Åland has been able to emerge somewhat in the international media sphere. Soccer is governed by the Åland Football Association (ÅFF), founded in 1943, which is a member of the Finnish Football Federation. These eleven clubs compete at various levels of Finnish soccer. IFK Mariehamn triumphed by winning the Veikkausliiga title in 2016. It was a historic victory for a modest Finnish club, but one that put the entire archipelago in the spotlight. The following year, IFK Mariehamn took part in the preliminary rounds of the Champions League. Women's club Åland United went even further, winning three championships (2009, 2013, 2020) and two Finnish Cups (2020, 2021), regularly qualifying for the Women's Champions League.

Nevertheless, many in Åland are pushing for the territory to be a true representation of their country's colors in one of the world's most popular sports, soccer. The recent accession of the British overseas territory of Gibraltar as a member of UEFA, and the long-standing membership of the Danish autonomous territory of the Faroe Islands in the European Football Association, attest to the fact that territories with a specific degree of autonomy can lay claim to international sporting representation in official competitions. Indeed, for the Faroe Islands, this integration has resulted in a sporting revolution: participation in genuine international matches, in qualifying rounds for European and world championships, and access to substantial financial resources. Gibraltar is now following suit, paving a promising path for the Åland archipelago to follow.

Åland's situation, with its autonomy and established footballing culture, could make it a candidate to join UEFA. "If others can, we can"[32]—this philosophy could well be the rallying cry that propels Åland to new footballing horizons.

---

32. PETTERSON Jörgen, Gibraltar lyckades där Åland gick snett, Nya Åland, December 17, 2015.

14. San Marino: Europe's "Smallest" Soccer Team

San Marino, one of the world's smallest and oldest states, uses its soccer team as a veritable ambassador to the international stage. Beyond the team's numerous defeats, football is above all a diplomatic means for this tiny country to promote its independence, acquired over 1,700 years ago.

Let's head for the Italian boot, home to one of the world's smallest states: San Marino, a territory of around 60 km2 and 34,000 inhabitants, landlocked in the middle of Italy. It's the third-smallest country in Europe, after the Vatican City and Monaco, and the fifth-smallest in the world. The territory may be tiny, but its history is rich. San Marino is without doubt the oldest republic in the world. Which, as we shall see, explains why this small country is so keen to have its soccer team promote the country.

For San Marino, it all began in the year 257. According to legend, the stonemason Marinus was involved in rebuilding the city walls of Rimini, after they had been destroyed by Liburnian pirates. He was unable to complete his work, however, as he was forced to flee the city following a wave of persecution launched against Christians by the Roman emperor Diocletian. Marinus built himself a refuge in the heights of Mount Titano, which later became a monastery where he lived as a hermit. As persecution continued, Christians came to seek refuge under the protection of this saintly Marinus. The birth date of San Marino is conventionally set for September 3, 301.

Over time, this small territory withstood various assaults and managed to preserve a degree of independence on its hilltops. It became a city republic, with its own legal code and constitution from 1600. San Marino thus claims to be the oldest existing sovereign state and constitutional republic. This particularity has been defended tooth and nail by the people of San Marino over the centuries, despite invasions, thanks to a skilful sense of diplomacy. Already during the Napoleonic Wars, the republic was recognized by Napoleon under the Treaty of Tolentino in 1797. Then, during the Italian wars of independence, San Marino took in one of the "fathers of the Italian fatherland", Giuseppe Garibaldi, thus avoiding being integrated into modern Italy in 1861. To secure its back, the small republic even wrote to the then President of the United States, Abraham Lincoln, proposing an alliance. This shrewd maneuver enabled San Marino to confirm its independence after signing a treaty of friendship with Italy in 1862. Since then, despite the turmoil and wars in Europe, San Marino has managed to preserve its independence and its republic. For the record, it is one of the few countries where a communist government was democratically elected to power, from 1945 to 1957.

But full autonomy isn't everything. To maintain its international profile, the country developed key sectors such as tourism, wine and stamps, and joined various international bodies. The small country became a state recognized by its peers, joining the Council of Europe in 1988 and the United Nations in 1992. The republic went even further, stepping up its sports diplomacy to promote its flag around the world. Already present at the Olympic Games since 1960, it joined UEFA and FIFA in 1988.

Soccer is one of San Marino's most popular sports, along with basketball and volleyball. The San Marino Football Federation was founded in 1931, followed very quickly by the first competition, the Coppa Titano, in 1936. It was only much later, in 1985, that soccer was really organized with the first official San Marino championship, featuring 15 teams. The national team, the *Serenissima*, was born a year later, in 1986, and played its first unofficial international match against the Canadian Olympic team, losing 1-0. It was a disappointment that was to be followed by many more after he joined various soccer organizations. In nearly 174 matches played, the San Marino national team has lost almost exclusively. The most notable of these was a crushing 13-0 defeat by Germany in the Euro 2008 qualifiers.

However, there is a golden age for the San Marino national team: the 1993 World Cup qualifiers. After a historic draw with Turkey, the team faced England on the final day. The match is an important one for the English, as a win with a large goal difference could qualify them for the World Cup in the USA. However, after 8'3" of play, San Marino opened the scoring. Davide Gualtieri made World Cup history by scoring the fastest goal of the qualifiers. It was an insignificant goal, as England went on to win 7-1, but it was a goal that made headlines around the world. As Gualtieri recalls, "the coach had told us to play the first ball right away, to attack, because we'd have very few opportunities during the match. In fact, the way the action unfolded left no room for doubt. This goal wasn't just a fluke"[33]. This feat transcends borders. In 1995, when San Marino travelled to Scotland, the Scots fans came to the stadium wearing shirts emblazoned with the words "Gualtieri—eight seconds".

Despite this achievement, San Marino will need a little luck to win their first match in official competition. To date, the national team has won just one match out of more than 170, in a friendly against Liechtenstein on April 28, 2004. Andy Selva, the *Serenissima*'s all-time top scorer and scorer of the winning free-kick, recalls: "The best goal was the one against Liechtenstein in 2004, synonymous with victory, the only one to date in the team's history."[34] This success was not repeated in official competition. As a result, the San Marino team, which has conceded almost 730 goals in its history against 24 scored, is still chasing its first victory. After the success against Liechtenstein, it was not until November 15, 2014, ten years later, that San Marino drew 0-0 at home against Estonia, thus ending a sequence of 61 defeats.

This catastrophic record is due to the fact that most San Marino players are not professionals, and find it difficult to play outside their homeland. This is why Andy Selva, one of the few San Marino players to have played at a high level in Italy, has set up the *Associazione Sammarinese Calciatori*, whose aim is to encourage the development of professionalism and to increase the resources of the soccer federation, which, for example, reimburses only 60 euros for the travel expenses of amateur players in the national team. For the time being, San Marino's soccer authorities are not naturalizing Italian players, despite requests from some of Italy's second- and third-division players.

---

33. Chadband Ian, "San Marino hero who humiliated England", *Evening Standard*, March 2003.
34. Pauluzzi Valentin, interview with Andy Sellva, *So Foot*, March 2015.

San Marino is currently ranked 210th in the FIFA world rankings, behind the British Virgin Islands and Anguilla. This places San Marino's national team in last place in world soccer. San Marino has even been overtaken in the rankings by European soccer's new minnows, Gibraltar. Nevertheless, the world's oldest republic is able to fly its flag and make a name for itself on the international stage thanks to its soccer and Olympic sporting events, despite the fact that the territory is only 60 km2 in size, equivalent to the town of Besançon.

As with other micro-states, San Marino has to find ways of cultivating its reputation. Sport is one of these levers. Soccer recently played a key role in the qualifiers for Euro 2020, where the national team's only goal, after 9 defeats and 46 goals conceded, was the subject of numerous press articles. One fan even sang the famous *Titanic* song *"My Heart Will Go On",* making it one of San Marino's most shared sporting exploits on the Internet. It's the Tokyo 2021 Olympic Games that will allow San Marino to shine, with their first 3 Olympic medals won.

As for participation in a possible Euro soccer tournament, it seems utopian, although a new competition, the League of Nations, enables "small" teams to gain access to this major European tournament. San Marino, for the moment, has no such objective, since its national team is the talk of the country "thanks" to its status as eternal loser. Sometimes it's better to be at the bottom of the table, rather than at the bottom of the pack.

Part Two: Beyond Europe

IV. Soccer:
a Battleground for States and Nations

15. Honduras-Salvador: the Soccer War

In 1969, Honduras and El Salvador, two neighboring Central American countries, were engaged in a political dispute. At the same time, their two national soccer teams were competing to qualify for the 1970 World Cup. These simple soccer matches, however, ignite flames that fan the embers of war between two "sister nations", whose respective governments do nothing but exacerbate their hatred of each other.

"If no football match had taken place in June 1969, another spark would surely have been found to ignite hostilities.[35] This observation by José M. Delgado, Rector of the University of San Salvador, sums up the heated context of the matches between Honduras and El Salvador in June 1969. These matches took place in such a poisonous climate that they were nicknamed "the soccer war".

Yet soccer was only the pretext for triggering the terrible conflict that ensued between Honduras and El Salvador, two neighboring Central American countries that share the same culture,

35. Ghemmour Chérif, *Terrain Miné, quand la politique s'immisce dans le soccer*, Hugo Sport, 2013, p. 132.

language and flag colors (blue and white). How could a soccer match, a popular celebration, become the catalyst for an almost fratricidal conflict? To answer this question, we need to delve into history. The two countries gained independence on the same day, September 15, 1821, and it was from the 1960s onwards that they took very different paths.

The demographic question is one of the main reasons for the deterioration in relations between the two countries. El Salvador, in the south, is one of the smallest countries in Central America, with a population of almost 4 million, or 200 inhabitants per km2. Honduras, to the north, has a population of 3 million over an area of 120,000 km2, or 25 inhabitants per km2. The Salvadoran population was so large that many emigrated to Honduran lands; by 1969, some 300,000 Salvadorans (10% of the total population of Honduras at the time) were working in their neighbor's fields. This massive exodus was due to the highly unequal distribution of land in El Salvador, as in Honduras, as we shall see later. At the time, El Salvador was controlled by an oligarchic regime, in the hands of "14 families"; 2% of the total population owned more than 60% of the land. The high level of immigration even prompted General Arrelano, who had seized power in Honduras following a coup d'état in 1963, to say, "The Salvadorans are colonizing Honduras!"

Yet the problems faced by the Honduran state have a name other than the spectre of foreigners: the United Fruit Company. This sprawling American multinational was a key player in Central America at the time. Its monopoly on the transport, sale and production of exotic produce meant that all countries had to go through the company, which gave it considerable leverage to make or break governments. In Honduras, the situation is such that the American company controls almost everything, from the ports to the railroads and banks. Its political and economic base enables it to change laws with bribes. This is where the expression "banana republic" comes from, coined by the American author O. Henry. He was referring to states whose economies are based exclusively on the production of exotic fruits, and whose survival depends on meeting the demands of multinationals. It's hard to resist when you know that, in 1975, for example, the United Fruit Company granted the Honduran leader, General Arrelano, the princely sum of $1.25 million, plus a promise of a further $1.25 million, in exchange for a reduction in banana export taxes.

This explains why, in 1962, the agrarian reform launched by the same Arrelano mainly benefited the large landowners and served the interests of United Fruit. The multinational's influence was considerable, as in 1966 it succeeded in bringing together a number of other large companies to create the National Federation of Honduran Farmers and Breeders (FENAGH), thus forging alliances with the wealthiest farmers in Honduras. The reform measures therefore fail to get to the heart of the problem of balancing land distribution. Salvadoran immigrants, also forced by their political power to emigrate for lack of available land, were clearly held responsible, and were gradually expelled from Honduras. Some of the vacant land is given to small farmers, who are still struggling financially and blame the Salvadorans for all their woes.

El Salvador, for its part, does not want its expelled nationals to return, as this would mean giving them land and, once again, amputating large Salvadoran landowners. Rather than finding a solution aimed at a better distribution of wealth, the two governments accuse each other. The territorial tension between the two neighbors had only just begun. The two authoritarian regimes set up a campaign of instrumentalization, with the aim of blaming national and agrarian problems on the neighboring state, and thus retaining power, while reinforcing the advantages granted to the United Fruit Company. It was against this stormy backdrop of heightened nationalist sentiment that El Salvador and Honduras met on a soccer pitch in June 1969.

The match was an important one, as the winner would be one step closer to a historic qualification for the World Cup, to be held the following year in Mexico. The first match, on June 8, 1969, was played at home for Honduras in Tegucigalpa. Honduras won 1-0 against an exhausted El Salvador team. It has to be said that the Salvadoran players were faced with numerous problems in the Honduran capital. After puncturing the tires of their bus, opposing fans prevented them from sleeping all night. Ryszard Kapuściński, a journalist at the time and author of the book *La Guerre du foot et autres guerres et aventures,* recounts: "The hotel was besieged by the crowd. The fans were whistling, screaming and shouting abuse. This went on all night. All this was done to make their exhausted and exasperated hosts lose the match.[36] At the same time, new expulsions of Salvadoran farmers are being carried out by the Honduran authorities.

On the soccer pitch, nothing is decided yet. Honduras needed one more match to qualify. But on June 15, 1969, it was El Salvador who defeated their neighbors 3-0 at home. Once again, conditions for the match were deplorable, with the Honduran players having to change hotels the night before, the first one having been set on fire. During these two matches, numerous acts of violence were committed on both sides, and many fans were injured, killed or raped... Worse still, after the first match, a young Salvadoran supporter, Amelia Bolanos,

36. Kapuściński Ryszard, *The Soccer War,* Granta Books, 1990.

shot herself in the heart in despair at seeing her team lose. A national funeral was held, and the Salvadoran authorities were quick to point the finger of blame at Honduras.

In this poisonous climate, soccer takes a back seat. Every match is an opportunity for each regime in power to stir up hatred of the neighboring country. In fact, a final match has to be played because, although El Salvador has scored more goals in both games, *goal-average is* not taken into account. This meant that a third match had to be played to decide between the two teams. It took place on June 26, 1969.

In view of the explosive situation, El Salvador broke off diplomatic relations with Honduras the day before. The match was therefore relocated to neutral ground in Mexico City. The match was played in a tense atmosphere, with supporters on both sides making it a matter of life and death. The players are no longer seen as sportsmen, but as soldiers armed with spikes who must avenge their humiliations. With Honduras leading 2-1, El Salvador finally prevailed in extra time, 3 goals to 2. Although the Salvadoran players were hailed as heroes, the sporting feat was quickly overshadowed by the fact that the victory was a tool for the two authoritarian powers.

After the match, the governments of both countries continued to fan the nationalist flames, leading to an increase in border incidents. On Monday July 14, 1969, the inevitable happened. A Salvadoran plane dropped a bomb in the Honduran capital, Tegucigalpa. The real war began. It's called the "Hundred Hours War". A short, almost fratricidal conflict, brought to a halt by pressure from the international community, but above all by the lack of arms and fuel in two exsanguinated countries. Nonetheless, in the space of a hundred hours, the war claimed between 3,000 and 6,000 lives, and wounded more than 15,000.

As a result, the El Salvador-Honduras conflict is infamously dubbed the "soccer war", following the book of the same name by Ryszard Kapuściński, in which he described the events. Football played only a minor role in this diplomatic escalation. For French anthropologist André-Marcel d'Ans, "[the] journalistic term 'soccer war' gives the impression that these are peoples ready to do battle over a simple ball. It's very devaluing, and this extremely violent war has undermined the potential of each country for a very long time"[37].

After this deadly conflict, the Salvadoran people had nothing to celebrate after El Salvador's historic participation in the 1970 World Cup—they had qualified after a final match against Haiti. The "Salvadoran heroes" performed no miracles in Mexico, losing all three of their matches against the host country, the USSR and Belgium, and failing to score a single goal.

On the diplomatic front, the authoritarian regimes remained in place, still riding the xenophobic wave, and did not sign a peace treaty until 1980. Apart from the fact that this war considerably strained relations between the two countries, it also halted the establishment of the Central American Common Market for 22 years, an economic union between Costa Rica, Guatemala, Honduras, Nicaragua and El Salvador that did little to please the interests of the United Fruit Company in the region.

Since then, Honduras and El Salvador have met on numerous occasions on the soccer field, but political tensions persist, with each political regime passing the buck to the neighbouring country, blaming it for its internal problems. It's as if history is repeating itself, yet again.

---

37. Ghemmour Chérif, *Terrain Miné, quand la politique s'immisce dans le soccer, op. cit.* p. 132.

16. When Hong Kong's Soccer Team Topples China

While China is tightening its laws on Hong Kong to make the territory fully Chinese, there was a time when Hong Kongers resisted Chinese hegemony through sport. This happened on May 19, 1985, on a soccer pitch. Such was China's humiliation that it (already) triggered a diplomatic row.

The Chinese vice is tightening around Hong Kong to make this territory, long British, a Chinese land in its own right. On May 28, 2020, the Parliament of the People's Republic of China passed a law on national security. A text which, according to the newspaper *Le Monde,* "puts an end to Hong Kong's democratic exception and considerably limits, if not annihilates, the civil and political liberties of any citizen who disagrees with the Chinese system"[38]. This explains the numerous protests by Hong Kongers, who have always emphasized their special status within China. Hong Kong's relative autonomy is increasingly challenged by China's central government.

38. De Changy Florence, "À Hongkong, la loi de sécurité imposée par la Chine met brutalement fin à une exception démocratique", *Le Monde,* July 2020.

The case of a soccer match is revealing in this respect. On May 19, 1985, a qualifying match for the 1986 Football World Cup pitted the two teams against each other. In 1985, Hong Kong was not yet under Chinese control. Since the Treaty of Nanking in 1842, Hong Kong had been a British colony. It wasn't until 1997 that the territory was handed back to China. Nevertheless, by the end of the 1970s, China had already set its sights on reclaiming the two major trading zones of Hong Kong, held by the United Kingdom, and Macau, under Portuguese control.

From 1978 onwards, China emerged from the long reign of Mao Zedong and sought to open up to the world with a series of economic reforms led by the new Party General Secretary, Deng Xiaoping. Initially, this opening-up was limited to special economic zones (SEZs). One of the first zones to benefit from these investments was the city of Shenzhen, located at the gateway to Hong Kong. It is experiencing spectacular growth. The Hong Kong territory, then an important economic center, became a strategic issue for the People's Republic of China. The United Kingdom, for its part, finds it difficult to see how it can preserve this territory, whose food supply is largely dependent on China.

On December 19 1984, an agreement was reached. The Sino-British Joint Declaration on the Question of Hong Kong was signed. Under the terms of this treaty, the UK would hand back Hong Kong, Kowloon and the New Territories to China on July 1, 1997. It was also with this treaty that the principle of "one country, two systems" began to be established for the 1997 handover. In other words, "socialism" as practiced in China would not be extended to Hong Kong, and the territory would enjoy a high degree of autonomy. Meanwhile, the Chinese state was also seeking to consolidate its international power in the sporting arena. Its comeback at the

1984 Olympic Games in Los Angeles saw it finish fourth among the nations with 32 medals.

After its return to the Olympic stage, China also wanted to enter the footballing arena by taking part in the World Cup. The 1982 edition came within a hair's breadth of success, after a 2-1 defeat to New Zealand in the final play-off match. Runners-up at the 1984 Asian Nations Cup, China were favourites to qualify for the 1986 World Cup in Mexico. Their qualifying group looked affordable, despite the presence of the disputed colonies of Hong Kong and Macau. China won their first group games without difficulty, beating Brunei and Macau, scoring 22 goals to 0 conceded.

However, to qualify, China had to play a final match against Hong Kong on May 19, 1985. The two teams had already met in the first leg and were unable to settle the tie at Hong Kong's Government Stadium. Before the final match, both teams had the same number of points. All it takes is a draw for the Chinese giants to qualify. China were favourites in this decisive match, having already beaten their opponents 2-0 in an Asian Cup qualifier six months earlier, and on several occasions in the qualifying stages for the 1982 World Cup. The Chinese Empire thus had its destiny in its own hands. At the same time, the Sino-British treaty was already beginning to exacerbate tensions between the two territories.

On May 5 1985, a fortnight before the match, the Hong Kong Seiko and Liaoning Province teams came to blows. The atmosphere became even more electrifying. The Hong Kong team took to the field at Beijing's Workers' Stadium, in front of more than 80,000 Chinese supporters. Yet it was Hong Kong's Cheung Chi Tak who scored the first goal, with a splendid free-kick from thirty yards. China were quick to respond, however, when Li Hui equalised 11 minutes later. Just as a draw would have qualified the Chinese, Hong

Kong's Ku Kam Fai extinguished their hopes on the hour mark. The Chinese team were unable to get back on level terms. On the pitch, the Hong Kong team officially qualified for the next round. In the stadium, the crowd goes wild, humiliated at having been beaten by the small British colony.

Thus began the riots of May 15, 1985, the first scene of protest caused by Chinese soccer. Debris was thrown into the stadium, hundreds of cars were set alight and the Chinese national team bus was overturned. It took the intervention of the Chinese police to stop the uprising, one of the worst incidents of public unrest in China since 1949. Tensions were so high that the Chinese team was confined for three days after the match. According to official sources, over 120 people were arrested. The president of the Chinese Football Association, Li Fenglou, and the coach of the national team, Zeng Xuelin, were forced to resign. The riots spread around the world. The *South China Morning Post* headlines: "Hong Kong victory sparks riots".[39]

For their part, the victorious Hong Kongers were given a hero's welcome. Some waved the Hong Kong flag of the day, while others displayed a banner with the slightly exaggerated words "Champions of Asia".

However, in the next round, the valiant Hong Kongers fell to Japan, 5-1 on aggregate, ending their hopes of playing in a World Cup. To this day, this epic achievement remains the Hong Kong soccer team's best performance in World Cup qualifying.

On the Chinese side, it was a cold shower. It wasn't until the 2002 World Cup in Japan and South Korea that the Chinese team

39. Wood Chris, "When Hong Kong beat China in a World Cup qualifier 32 years ago, and riots that followed", *South China Morning Post*, May 2017.

took part in the first World Cup in its history. But China is slow to become a nation that counts in the world's most popular sport. Even so, for several years now, Xi Jinping, President of the People's Republic of China, has been making every effort to ensure that the Chinese team and players become major players on the footballing planet, with the ambitious goal of winning a World Cup by 2050.

After the events of 1985, Hong Kong and China met again on the soccer field, notably in the 2018 World Cup qualifiers. Both matches ended in draws, and neither team managed to qualify. In Hong Kong, the historic May 19 match is still celebrated, and on its anniversary in 2015, a commemorative match is even held to celebrate the thirtieth anniversary of the historic 1985 victory.

Today, the battle is being waged on an entirely different terrain, as China wants to bring Hong Kong fully back under its authority, even if it means using the hard way by imposing a National Security Law that considerably restricts the Hong Kong exception. The issue has even slipped into the international arena, with the European Union and the United States condemning this Chinese "offensive", perceived by its detractors as an attack on individual freedoms and the territory's autonomy. The noose is tightening, however, as at the start of 2021, Beijing tightened its grip on Hong Kong, with a reform of the electoral system further restricting the voice of opponents. This grip is confirmed in 2024, when a new law on Hong Kong's national security is passed, firmly condemning treason, insurrection and espionage, and putting an end to many of the legal guarantees enjoyed by Hong Kong, in order to bring it into line with legislation in mainland China.

17. Argentina-England: Maradona Avenges the Falklands War

The Falkland Islands have been claimed for centuries by Argentina and the United Kingdom. This territorial issue was at the heart of a legendary match at the 1986 World Cup. The main protagonist was the recently deceased soccer star Diego Armando Maradona.

"It was as if we'd beaten a country, not just a soccer team. Although we said before the match that soccer had nothing to do with the Falklands War, we knew [that the English] had shot a lot of young Argentinians like little birds. So this match was revenge."[40] With these words, taken from his autobiography, *Yo Soy El Diego*[41], legendary footballer Diego Armando Maradona describes what went on behind the scenes of Argentina's victory over England on June 22, 1986. This soccer match was much more than just a match, given the tense diplomatic context between the two countries. At the heart of the conflict were the Falklands.

40. Ghemmour Chérif, *Terrain Miné, quand la politique s'immisce dans le soccer, op. cit.* p. 172.
41. Maradona Diego Armando, *Yo Soy El Diego,* Planeta, 2001.

It's a small archipelago of around 3,500 inhabitants, off the coast of Patagonia and Argentina. Yet this territory of 12,000 km2, the size of Qatar, is British for the time being. Throughout history, many countries have fought to conquer these islands, including France, Spain and the United Kingdom. In 1816, Argentina became independent and took over Spanish claims to the islands. Given its strategic position, the United Kingdom did its utmost to reconquer the Falklands in 1833 and gradually establish settlements there. Since then, Argentina has claimed sovereignty over the territory, which it calls the *Malvinas*, while the United Kingdom calls the Falkland Islands.

This situation created a climate of tension between Argentina and the United Kingdom. Although the two countries began negotiations in 1965, following the implementation of the United Nations Declaration on the Granting of Independence to Colonial Countries and Peoples, the situation remained deadlocked. It took a different turn the following years, when Argentina was under military dictatorship. All means were used to conceal the country's serious economic and political problems. The government struggled to unify the country, which had been suffering violent political and social unrest for over 30 years, leading to the establishment of a military dictatorship by General Videla in 1976. This new authoritarian political regime did not allow Argentina to recover, although the political instrumentalization of the 1978 Football World Cup on home soil sought to give the country a better international image.

In search of legitimacy in the eyes of the population (annual inflation at the time was 140%) and guided by expansionist ambitions, the military junta, now led by General Galtieri, launched the seductive "Bicontinental Argentina" project, aimed at enabling the country to expand as far as Antarctica and become an undisputed regional power. All the more reason to strengthen national sentiment. The Falklands are the ideal starting point for this project of conquest, as they represent a gateway to Antarctica and are already highly symbolic in the Argentine imagination.

And so, on April 2, 1982, Operation Rosario began: Argentine soldiers launched an offensive against the British archipelago. It was a risky gamble, but Argentina's political powers were banking on the fact that the alliance between Argentina and the United States would protect the country from a possible rout. The Conservatives in power in London, led by their Prime Minister Margaret Thatcher, were taken by surprise by this military attack, which contradicted their intelligence. The government was initially accused of negligence. The "Iron Lady" strikes back, building her legend with a military response in less than a week. After just two months of fighting, on June 14, after 649 Argentine and 255 British deaths, the Argentine armed forces were forced to sign the peace treaty. In Argentina, this final defeat precipitated the end of the military dictatorship; the first democratic presidential election, in 1983, brought Raúl Alfonsín to power. On the British side, Thatcher was strengthened by this victory, which she followed up with electoral success.

Three years later, in 1986, the two democracies, still at loggerheads over diplomatic issues, emerged as serious contenders for victory at the Football World Cup in Mexico. Diego Armando Maradona, 26, was at the top of his game, and was also the leader of a solid *Albiceleste,* the Argentine national team, while his English counterpart boasted a number of in-form stars such as Gary Lineker and Bryan Robson. After a relatively uneventful group stage, both teams impressed in the Round of 16, where they beat Uruguay (1-0) and Paraguay (3-0) respectively. On June 22, in

Mexico City's stadium, the two nations met for the first time since the Falklands confrontation.

The confrontation brings back other painful memories for the Argentinians. At the 1966 World Cup, held on British soil, the quarter-final between England and Argentina turned into a pitched battle. The expulsion of Argentine captain Antonio Rattin set off a firestorm. The player contested the decision and took ten minutes to leave the pitch, in the process tearing the British flag from the corner post. This confused situation gave rise to the red card, which directly expels a player from the match. The match was no longer a sporting affair. After England's 1-0 victory, against a backdrop of refereeing complacency, the *British* coach, Alf Ramsey, prevented his players from exchanging shirts.

This stormy historical context is spiced up by the sulphurous statements made by Argentine players prior to the 1986 match. Nery Pumpido, Argentina's goalkeeper, warned: "Beating the English will be a double satisfaction for what happened in the Falklands."[42] *The Sun* announces "the landing of 5,000 men"[43] in reference to the English fans who have made the trip.

It's midday in Mexico City, the heat is stifling, and English flags finish burning in the stands housing 115,000 people. A legendary match is about to begin. The confrontation is warlike, rough. The British side's instructions were clear: leave no space for the prodigy Maradona, and dissuade him from keeping the ball. The Argentinian No.10 was not spared, and the first half, pleasant though it was, ended goalless. But as soon as the half-time whistle sounded, in the 51st minute, the first shot was fired.

42. Carlin John, "England vs Argentina—A history", *The Guardian*, May 2002.
43. *Ibid.*

When the ball was badly cleared and English goalkeeper Peter Shilton's clearance was poor, Maradona threw himself forward, jumped and touched the ball with his left hand to score. The referee, Mr. Bennaceur, guided by his assistant and impeccable throughout this stormy encounter, made an obvious error: the goal was validated, the *Mano de Dios* ("hand of God") was born. Three minutes later, the *Pibe de Oro* scored another masterly goal, this time in accordance with the rules. 10 seconds, 50 metres, 6 players eliminated: Maradona scored the *Gol del Siglo* ("Goal of the Century"), much to the delight of an Argentine commentator on the verge of orgasm, who described it live as a "cosmic kite". England's Gary Lineker went so far as to say that it was the only time in his career that he felt like applauding an opponent's goal.

He headed home the winner in the 81st minute, but the fate of the match was sealed: Argentina, thanks to a diabolically brilliant Maradona, eliminated England. The Argentinian would later say: "We said we shouldn't mix soccer and politics, but that was a lie. I got my hands on the ball to take revenge on the English for getting their hands on the Falklands.

The Argentinian star, who scored twice against the Belgians in the semi-final, led his team to the title, which they won 3-2 over Germany, and was the tournament's best player (5 goals, 5 assists).

Since then, several matches have served as reminders of the rivalry between the two countries. In 1991, at Wembley, Maradona came out onto the pitch ostensibly holding the ball in his left hand. In 2002, during a World Cup clash, the Argentine anthem was loudly whistled by English fans. At the 1998 World Cup in France, players from both teams almost came to blows. England's David Beckham lost his temper with the ebullient Diego Simeone, before the Argentinians finally won the game after a heated penalty shoot-out.

Although the last time the two countries met was in 2005, the geopolitical conflict is still present. Tensions are being rekindled by Argentina's lavish commemoration of its thirtieth anniversary in 2012, and by the anti-British rhetoric of Cristina Kirchner (president of Argentina from 2007 to 2015). Why so much virulence from both countries for such a small archipelago? Control of fishing zones is one factor, but it is above all the discovery, in 2010, of a 350 million-barrel oil field in relatively shallow waters that has rekindled tensions around the archipelago. Beyond the financial aspect, the Falklands form an interesting anchorage point for the UK at a time when the South American continent is beginning to emerge; moreover, the conflict has made the archipelago a symbol of British resistance abroad, far from its bases. The inhabitants are in any case attached to the British Crown, as they voted in a referendum in March 2013 for the territory to remain British, with almost 99.8% of the vote.

Be that as it may, the Anglo-Argentine rivalry, on and off the pitch, is not over. Although the two governments reached an agreement in 2016 to boost growth there, the Brexit is plunging this British overseas territory into uncertainty. This reopens the question of sovereignty over these islands. The arrival in power in Argentina of the populist and whimsical Javier Milei will not revive a calm diplomatic debate on the subject, since he has asserted throughout his campaign that "Argentina's sovereignty over the Falkland Islands is non-negotiable".

18. Qatar-Saudi Arabia: Soccer's New Duel?

In the space of just a few decades, the small Middle Eastern emirate has become a major player in world sport, with soccer taking center stage. So much so, in fact, that it has acquired the Paris-Saint-Germain football club, established a presence in the world of sports media through the BeIn Media Group network, and secured the organization of one of the world's greatest sporting events, the 2022 World Cup. With the aim, through sport, of growing Qatar, putting it on the map and being identified as a key international player. These successes have ended up irritating its great regional rival, Saudi Arabia, which for some years has been seeking to imitate the Qatari strategy in order to benefit from the "positive" effects of this sporting soft power.

In 2022, Qatar and its 11,000 km2 of land hosted one of the world's greatest sporting events, the Football World Cup. Quite a feat, considering that previous editions have been hosted by much larger countries in terms of size: Russia in 2018, Brazil in 2014, and South Africa in 2010. Because, yes, Qatar is tiny by global standards, comparable in size to the Île-de-France region. This Middle Eastern nation has a population of just 2.5 million, of whom only 10% are nationals. This fragile demographic configuration is compounded by the presence of its large neighbor and rival: Saudi Arabia, with its 2,000,000 km2, is the 13th largest country in the world. Yet it was the small Qatari territory that became the first Arab country to host a FIFA World Cup. A coup for the Gulf state, which already owns the Paris-Saint-Germain football club and has a strong presence in the sporting world, thanks in particular to its BeIn Sports media group and its various sponsors. With such a strong presence in the sporting arena, Qatar aims to make its mark on the world stage.

Indeed, this country gained its independence less than 50 years ago, in 1971. It soon had to find ways of extricating itself from the influence, and even interference, of its neighbors, in particular the powerful Saudis. It was not until 1995, under the leadership of Emir Hamad ben Khalifa Al Thani, that Qatar broke away from its tutelage to fully exist on the international stage. Aided, it's true, by the revenues derived from the exploitation of its gas-rich subsoil to support its strategy of influence. Qatar then set about gaining power in the region. In 1996, the Qatari government launched the Al Jazeera news channel, with the aim of breaking the Saudi monopoly on Arab media. This strategy of influence is better known as *soft power*, as opposed to hard power, which uses more coercive means.

To consolidate this power, win over the international community and preserve its territorial integrity in the face of its powerful neighbors, Qatar was quick to rely on sport and its universal values. As Sheikh Ahmed Ben Abdallah Al-Sulaîti, CEO of Qatar National Broadband Network, recalls in L'Équipe newspaper, "Saudi Arabia is the country of oil, Bahrain the hub of finance, Dubai the hub of trade. To exist on the international stage, Qatar had the choice of industry and sport. And sport is the ideal vector"[44]. The problem was that the emirate was far from being a sporting nation in the 1990s, despite having been a member of FIFA since 1970. Nevertheless, the Gulf state invested heavily to become a global sports powerhouse. The first stone in the building of this future empire was the organization of an international tennis tournament in the capital, Doha, in 1993. This was soon followed by participation in equestrian, sailing, motor sports and golf competitions, and the organization of the first major competition to bring together numerous national delegations, the 2006 Asian Games.

This ambitious diplomacy through sport has gradually moved on to more mainstream sports. The first of these is soccer. Qatar's entry into the world of football came on December 2, 2010, when it was awarded the contract to host the 2022 World Cup. This came as something of a surprise, given that the Emirate is far from being a traditional footballing nation, especially as it had to contend with a bid from the United States. However, since the early 2000s, the Emirate has been working behind the scenes within the sport's governing bodies to gain influence. It came as such a surprise that the vote for the award was the subject of numerous suspicions of corruption within FIFA, as revealed in the book *The Man Who Bought a World Cup. The Qatari Conspiracy*[45], by journalists Heidi Black and Jonathan Calvert. Suspicions were confirmed by an FBI investigation and the Garcia report on the controversial awarding of the 2018 and 2022 World Cups to Russia and Qatar respectively. The institution of FIFA was shaken by its affairs, which led in particular

44. Guégan Jean-Baptiste, *Géopolitique du sport, une autre explication du monde*, Bréal, 2017, p. 165.
45. Blake Heidi and Calvert Jonathan, *The Ugly Game: The Qatari Plot to Buy the World Cup*, Simon&Chuster, 2016.

to the resignation of its president, Sepp Blatter, as well as the arrest of several of the organization's top executives in 2015. However, the 2022 World Cup will still be awarded to Qatar, despite the numerous criticisms and controversies surrounding the economic and human costs of this World Cup, as well as calls for a boycott, mostly from Western countries.

In geopolitical terms, this Qatari consecration puts a terrible strain on relations in the Middle East. Especially with Saudi Arabia, which sees its "small" neighbor and former pre-square gain in global prestige. Relations between these two states have been deteriorating since the early 2010s, with the emergence of the Arab Spring, with both countries supporting different sides. Diplomatic escalation culminated in a blockade of Qatar by Saudi Arabia and its allies in 2017, with Riyadh accusing its rival of supporting terrorist organizations and close ties with the region's other major power, Iran. Despite the large-scale presence and threats of military attack, Qatar has managed to keep its economy afloat and mobilize the international community around its case. Its political and sporting influence is no small part of this. Worse still, the blockade undermined the region's already precarious economic balance. Since then, relations have tended to warm up, although Qatar's ever-increasing role in world sporting bodies has irritated its large neighbor. The situation calmed down at the beginning of 2021, when Saudi Arabia lifted the blockade.

Qatar's *success story*, thanks to its sports diplomacy, is giving ideas to the Saudi petromonarchy. Indeed, since the early 2010s, Saudi Arabia has been seeking to modernize and diversify its economy, which is ultra-dependent on fossil fuels (31% of its GDP and 79% of its export revenues in 2018). Problem: between the affair of critical Saudi journalist Jamal Khashoggi, murdered inside the Saudi consulate in Istanbul in 2017, and the controversial military intervention in Yemen since 2015, not to mention accusations of human rights abuses, Saudi Arabia's image has deteriorated considerably over the years. As for women's rights, although Saudi women now have the right to drive and have a national championship, they are virtually non-existent, since they remain legally under the guardianship of their "guardian"—father, husband or son.

What better way than sport to modernize the monarchy's image and attract foreign investors to diversify its economy? At the same time, it can reinforce its regional dominance in the Persian Gulf, by not letting Qatar get too far ahead of it. It is therefore through sport that Saudi Arabia has chosen to restore its image. This sporting *soft power is* part of a more global strategy, dubbed Vision 2030. Launched in 2016, this plan is the brainchild of Crown Prince Mohammed bin Salmane, then Minister of Defense, who now holds the country's reins. Vision 2030 aims to modernize the Saudi regime by multiplying international partnerships, strengthening services to the population, modernizing institutions and investing in key sectors such as sustainable development, new technologies and tourism.

Qatar, however, is well ahead of the game. Already in the early 2000s, the Qatar Foundation logo appeared on the shirts of one of the world's most popular clubs, FC Barcelona. Above all, on May 31, 2011, the Qatari state investment fund Qatar Sport Investment (QSI) bought the Paris-Saint-Germain club for 70 million euros. A strategic choice, not only to restore a club with a long history on the national and European scene, but also to associate Qatar with the world's most visited city, Paris, and thus gain in visibility. In ten years, thanks to Qatari investment, PSG has become one of soccer's biggest brands, with almost 75 million fans worldwide. Qatar has also been able to leverage the reputation of international stars such as David Beckham, Neymar, Leo Messi and Kylian Mbappé, recruited at a premium. The Gulf state can also draw on its *BeIn Media Group* sports channel network, created in 2011, which is present in over 40 countries on five continents and is considered the world's largest buyer of sports rights.

Long in the shadow of the region's other oil states and their ambitious sports policies, the Saudi regime has shifted gears in 2019 to attract sporting event organizers and fans from around the world. Since the $100 million *"Clash of Dunes"* boxing match between stars Anthony Joshua and Andy Ruiz in 2019, the Saudi state has been hosting more and more prestigious sporting events on its soil. Like the Formula 1 Grand Prix, to match its neighbors Bahrain and the United Arab Emirates for a renowned motor race.

Saudi Arabia has also succeeded in securing the Dakar Rally and the organization of a cycling tour on its soil in 2020. These competitions will not only attract foreign advertisers, but will also showcase the country's landscapes, bringing Saudi Arabia to a global audience. As Carole Gomez, research director in the geopolitics of sport at the IRIS Institute, explains, "the idea is to showcase the beauty of the landscapes, the infrastructures that can welcome you if you come on a trip, and to make a postcard of Saudi Arabia"[46]. Since opening its borders to foreign tourists in September 2019, the Saudi state has issued 400,000 visas. The country now intends to do much more. In soccer, Saudi Arabia doesn't have a World Cup like its Qatari neighbor, but it is starting to become a destination of choice for other competitions, such as

46. GOMEZ Carole, "Le sport, un levier d'influence pour l'Arabie Saoudite", RFI interview, January 2020.

the Italian and Spanish Supercups, which pit recognized European teams against each other.

Always with a view to extending its influence and competing with its "media" neighbors, the Saudi state is looking to invest in a European club. Initial rumors suggested that Saudi Arabia wanted to buy Manchester United, which would have been a way of entering the world of soccer through the front door, since the English club is the third richest in the world, with over 130 million fans worldwide, and has sales of over 700 million euros for 2018/2019. Not an insignificant choice, given that the other club in the English metropolis, Manchester City, is owned by Sheikh Mansour, a member of the Abu Dhabi royal family.

The deal was too big for the Saudi state, which set its sights on another, more affordable English club in 2019: Newcastle United. A takeover for over 300 million euros that will only take place once Saudi Arabia has lifted its blockade on Qatar. Indeed, before the blockade was lifted, the takeover was blocked because BeIN Sport, the Premier League's main international TV rights holder, claimed that the Saudi investment ran counter to English interests, as Saudi Arabia was pirating the Qatari group's channels. The resumption of diplomatic relations put an end to the piracy and unblocked the situation so that Saudi Arabia could also have its own soccer team. The purchase was made possible by Saudi Arabia's sovereign investment fund, the PIF (Public Investment Fund). Weighing in at over $600 billion, this fund supports Saudi investments in its Vision 2030 plan, including those in sport.

Qatar's objective remains to establish itself as the central sporting nation of the 21st century. The Qatar Olympic Committee has set itself the ambitious goal of staging 50 international competitions by 2030. This is already underway, with the staging of world championships in handball in 2015, cycling in 2016, athletics in 2019 and swimming in 2023... And why not, at a later date, the Olympic Games? The emirate's influence not only serves to make it shine, but also to diversify an economy dependent on the exploitation of fossil fuels. Like its Saudi neighbor.

In any case, the 2022 World Cup illustrated the relative détente in diplomatic relations between the two countries: an event at which the Emir of Qatar, Tamim Al Thani, and the Saudi Crown Prince, Mohammed Ben Salmane, appeared together to illustrate a renewed unity to promote investment in the Persian Gulf and turn it into a hub for global sport. Building on this momentum, Saudi Arabia continues to deploy a strategy of massive investment in sport, targeting soccer in particular with the transformation of its local league, the Saudi Pro League, thanks to the arrival of global stars such as Cristiano Ronaldo, Neymar, Karim Benzema and Sadio Mané. This ambitious strategy aims to raise the standard of the domestic league by equipping the kingdom's four biggest teams with world-class players, while ensuring a balanced distribution of talent across the league. Furthermore, the privatization and corporatization of emblematic clubs (Al Ittihad, Al Ahli, Al Nassr and Al Hilal), under the aegis of the Sovereign Investment Fund (PIF) and non-profit foundations, reflects Saudi Arabia's determination to invest without limit to make the Saudi Pro League a competitor to the biggest soccer leagues and a showcase for the country.

Beyond soccer, Saudi Arabia is expanding its footprint in world sport, becoming a major sponsor of Formula 1 via Aramco and managing to merge the world golf circuit with the establishment of the LIV Golf Series. These initiatives, combined with large-scale projects such as NEOM, a futuristic city destined to become a showcase for Saudi modernity and innovation and which will host the

2029 Asian Winter Games, and FIFA's award of the 2034 World Cup, confirm the kingdom's ambition to become a key player on the global sporting stage.

This regional dynamic raises questions about the future of rivalry and cooperation between Qatar and Saudi Arabia. For the time being, the two countries seem to be taking a complementary approach, capitalizing on their respective assets to strengthen their sporting and geopolitical influence, but could the scale of their ambitions once again inflame their relations? The Middle East is asserting itself as the next great territory of world sport, but the question remains: how far will this "joint" sporting-political ambition take Qatar and Saudi Arabia? And what form will their rivalry take in the future?

V. Soccer as a Means of Emancipating People

19. 1958-1962:
Algeria's "Eleven of Independence

With the Algerian war in full swing in 1958, the Algerian National Liberation Front (FLN) came up with the idea of creating a soccer team to mobilize French and international opinion for the country's independence. This team was much more than a simple selection. With its prowess on and off the pitch, this "Eleven of Independence", with its uninhibited and spectacular style of play, would travel the world in the name of a free Algeria.

"By your actions, you have advanced the revolution by ten years.[47] These were the words of Ferhat Abbas, the first head of state of the Algerian Republic, when he met the Algerian National Liberation Front (FLN) soccer team in 1961. This team, mainly made up of professional players, toured the world to promote the issue of Algerian independence internationally.

After the Second World War, Algerian territory remained under French control since 1830. However, the Algerian colony was

47. Correia Mickaël, *Une histoire populaire du soccer,* La découverte, 2018, p. 161.

declared an integral part of France by the Constitution of 1848, and divided into three departments (Algiers, Oran and Constantine). Over the years, the movement for Algerian independence grew, leading to the creation of the Union populaire algérienne party in 1938 and the Manifeste du peuple algérien in 1943. The situation reached a point of no return on May 8, 1945, with the Sétif massacre, during which the French armed forces bloodily suppressed nationalist demonstrations. From that date onwards, the independence movement gained considerable momentum.

Two events accelerated the process. Firstly, the Arab revolution in Egypt in 1952, which put an end to the British occupation. Secondly, the defeat of the French army at Diên Biên Phu in 1954, which brought the Indochina War to an end and symbolized the decline of the former French colonial empire. Following these events, France embarked on a process of decolonization, culminating in the independence of Morocco and Tunisia in 1956. This was not the case for Algeria, as France considered this territory to be an integral part of metropolitan France—its subsoil, rich in fossil resources, especially gas, was a significant strategic asset.

On November 1, 1954, FLN armed forces launched some 70 attacks on French strategic points. This event, known as All Saints' Day, marked the start of the Algerian War of Independence. The conflict intensified from 1956 onwards, with some 450,000 French soldiers mobilized to fight against 25,000 Algerian *fellagas*. However, the conflict received little media coverage. The UN was slow to recognize Algeria's right to self-determination. France, for its part, described the situation as an internal police problem. To emphasize that the conflict was virtually non-existent, French Cup matches were organized on Algerian soil. And yet, it was thanks to football that FLN leaders tried to find ways of publicizing their struggle for Algerian independence.

The idea began to emerge in 1956: to use the large contingent of professional Algerian players in metropolitan France (nearly thirty) to form a soccer team. Some of them were already supporting the cause by paying a revolutionary tax, representing up to 15% of their salary. The aim of this selection is to make the FLN team the standard-bearer of Algerian independence and an ambassador for the future country in building future international relations.

Mohamed Boumezrag, a former professional player and director of the Algerian regional sub-division of the French Football Federation (FFF), prepared the ground in 1957 by meeting several of the footballers likely to join such a project. On April 13, 1958, 9 Algerian footballers deserted their first division clubs. Among them was Mustapha Zitouni, a key figure in the French national team, as well as players like Abdelaziz Ben Tifour, Mohamed Maouche and the young hopeful Rachid Mekhloufi, who were regularly called up by Les Bleus. The shockwave was such that the following day, the newspaper *L'Équipe ran the* headline: "Nine Algerian footballers have disappeared".[48] A major blow for the clubs, and above all for the French national soccer team, which a month later had to start preparing for the 1958 World Cup. It was also a powerful symbol, since few public figures have been involved in the Algerian question until now. As Rachid Mekhloufi explains, "[few] French people knew what was happening in Algeria. The French people became aware when we left that there was an Algerian war, a war of liberation"[49].

All the players arrived in Tunisia on May 9, 1958. Barely a month after their flight, the Front de Libération Nationale team played its first match against Morocco at the Chedly-Zouiten stadium in

48. *Ibid*, p. 156.
49. *Ibid*, p. 157.

Tunis. For the first time, the colors of independent Algeria were waved in a stadium, and the Algerian anthem was sung at the top of one's lungs. This first match was also the first victory for the team soon dubbed the "Eleven of Independence". Two days later, it was the *same story*: victory over Tunisia. The French reaction was swift, with FIFA deciding, under pressure from the FFF, to suspend the defectors and sanction any federation or team that agreed to meet them officially. In the end, this led to much more attention being paid to the banned nomadic squad of up to 32 players. As Mustapha Zitouni explains, "[our] departure showed that the entire Algerian population was with the FLN, not just bandits and mercenaries. We were happy in France, we had situations, the people loved us. We weren't against France, but against colonialism, against the people who were in Algeria and had monopolized the country's assets"[50].

Despite the sanctions, during its four years of existence the Algerian national team competed against a number of clubs and national teams, often under a different name. From May to July 1959, the Algerian team embarked on its first international tour of Eastern Europe, as the USSR and the Soviet bloc looked favorably on any independent movement that might weaken the Western bloc countries. For the FLN, these international matches between its team and those of "brotherly countries" were intended to foreshadow the future diplomatic relations of independent Algeria. Even if, on paper, the team plays against local teams, these are in fact the real national teams on the pitch. At every match, the Algerian team makes no attempt to hide its identity, and insists that these symbols are very much in evidence. This has led to tensions with

50. *Ibid*, p. 158.

the Polish team, who agreed to play against the "Algerian Eleven" after the team threatened to boycott the match.

This European tour is impressive. The footballers played in a free spirit, in the image of the emancipation movement they wished to defend. On the pitch, the FLN team's soccer illustrates the collective emancipation aspirations of the Algerian people. Their style of play paid off, with an average of 4 goals per game and a significant number of victories. In October 1959, the national team continued its media campaign, flying out to Southeast Asia for a dozen matches in China and North Vietnam. There, just after a match against a Vietnamese team, General Vo Nguyên Giap, victor of the battle of Diên Biên Phu, told the Algerian players: "We beat the French, and you beat us in soccer. So you're going to beat France.[51]

The team reached its peak on March 29, 1961 in Belgrade, inflicting a real beating on the Yugoslavian team, finalists in the 1960 Euro, with a 6-1 victory, watched by the French ambassador in the audience. The "Eleven of Independence" continued its journey until the signing of the Evian agreements between the French government and the provisional government of the Algerian Republic. These agreements put an end to the war and paved the way for Algeria's independence, officially proclaimed on July 5, 1962. As for soccer, suspensions were lifted and Algerian players could return to play for French clubs. After four years of touring the world, often in precarious conditions, the FLN team played nearly 91 matches, winning 65, drawing 13 and losing 13, and played a key role in Algeria's future diplomatic relations.

---

51. GHEMMOUR Chérif, *Terrain Miné, quand la politique s'immisce dans le soccer, op. cit.* p. 98.

20. Greenland: Football as a New Route to Independence

For some years now, Greenland, the world's largest island, has been plotting its course towards independence from Denmark. Although the Danish authorities are not totally against the idea, the climatic, diplomatic and economic obstacles to achieving it are numerous. Soccer, the country's most popular sport, could well be the ice-breaker over these obstacles to greater autonomy.

"In Greenland, soccer connects everyone. We want to show that even though we're a small nation with so few inhabitants, we can play soccer at a high level."[52] Patrick Frederiksen, captain of one of Greenland's leading clubs, B-67, has a point. Football is quite simply the most popular sport in the country, where almost 10% of the population play. For some years now, soccer has been a formidable tool of emancipation for this large country on the Arctic frontier.

Greenland may be an immense island of over 2 million km2, but its geographical location between the Arctic and Atlantic oceans

52. Ward Tom, "The inside story of Greenland's one-week soccer season", *Red Bull*, November 2019.

means that the territory is subject to severe climatic constraints, forcing its 55,000 inhabitants to live on a narrow coastal strip. A "small" nation in a large territory, which continues to attract covetousness. Indeed, global warming is accelerating glacier melt, which increased 4-fold between 2003 and 2013. Despite this ominous scenario, the opening up of new trade routes is opening up opportunities for this too-often forgotten territory.

It's true that, in the past, Greenland's location and climate haven't exactly helped attract the curious. And yet, according to legend, the country's name, which means "green land", was given by Icelandic explorers to attract settlers to these hostile lands. It wasn't until the Second World War that the island's strategic position began to attract interest. Denmark was occupied by Nazi Germany, and Greenland, which had been a Danish territory since 1814, could follow suit. They therefore turned the Arctic territory into a forward base. At the end of the war, the Americans offered to buy the island from Denmark for $100 million. The offer was refused, although the American presence remained, with a major military base in the town of Thule, integrated into NATO in 1951. As for Denmark, it opened Greenland to free trade and changed its status from colony to Danish province in 1953.

From then on, the Danish government implemented a policy of cultural assimilation towards the Greenlanders. As time went on, a movement for greater Greenlandic autonomy began to develop in the 1970s. What's more, due to the political complications associated with Denmark's entry into the European Common Market in 1972, the search began for a different status for Greenland. As a result, Greenland was granted internal self-government status in 1979, with the creation of a parliament and a government with sovereignty over domestic matters. In 1985, Greenland successfully withdrew from the European Economic Community, by referendum, to protect its fishing grounds, while Denmark remained a member. The differentiation became more pronounced, as it was also at this time that Greenland adopted its own flag, red and white, which, according to its creator Thue Christiansen, represents the sun on the sea and icebergs drifting on the waves, and uses the Danish colors.

In 2009, this autonomy was reinforced following a referendum. Greenland is now co-sovereign in the management and exploitation of its subsoil resources, and Greenlandic becomes the official language. The country also has a constitutional right to self-determination, with the backing of Denmark. The road to independence seemed to be taking shape: in 2016, the coalition government led by Prime Minister Kim Kielsen announced the creation of a Ministry for Independence. The coalition agreement begins with the words: "Greenland is irrevocably on the road to independence."[53]

However, this road is far from completely clear, as the territory is so economically dependent on Denmark. Despite its enormous mineral resources, the island's economy still relies exclusively on fishing and on economic aid from Denmark, to the tune of 500 million euros, which represents 60% of Greenland's budget. With its extreme temperatures, vast distances and lack of infrastructure, exploiting the hydrocarbon-rich subsoil is still extremely complex. Only two mines are currently in operation in the south of the island. These dim economic prospects are not, therefore, driving Greenlanders to immediate independence, as they fear a drop in their standard of living.

53. Smith Rory, "Soccer at the Edge of the World", *The New York Times*, September 2019.

Independence therefore requires economic autonomy, with major investment in infrastructure to exploit fossil resources and diversify the economy, taking inspiration, for example, from the Icelandic model of developing local ecological tourism. The appetites of mining companies and governments are numerous around Greenland and its subsoil. China and the United States, in particular, have their sights set on the island's uranium deposits and strategic position.

Soccer can be a lever for independence and international recognition, helping to make the region more attractive. Despite the climatic conditions, football is one of the island's most popular sports, with almost 5,000 licensed players—almost 10% of the population—and almost 70 clubs across the island. A championship has also been held since 1954, but the climate is such that it is played over a week. In 2019, to qualify for one of the 8 places in the tournament, 40 teams from all over the country took part in regional qualifiers. The development of soccer is supported by Greenland's political authorities to promote sporting activities, and thus reduce social problems linked to alcoholism or suicides.

The country's soccer organization has a long history: a Greenland Football Association was founded in 1971, the first step towards building a national team. The team played its first international match on July 2, 1980, against the Faroe Islands, losing 6-0. After several more matches against neighboring countries, Greenland began the process of becoming a member of FIFA in 1998, in order to take part in the World Cup qualifiers. This process was far from far-fetched, since the world soccer organization accepts into its ranks countries that are not completely independent. This is the case, for example, of the Faroe Islands, also an autonomous territory of Denmark, which have been members of FIFA since 1988, and of UEFA since 1990.

To back up its claim, Greenland organizes international matches. The team made news on June 30, 2001, when it played Tibet in Copenhagen. The match attracted international attention when China threatened to embargo Greenland's shrimp exports because of Tibet's disputed sovereignty. Despite Chinese pressure, the match went ahead in Copenhagen's Vanløse stadium. Nearly 5,000 fans attended this historic meeting between two representatives of territories not recognized at international level. Greenland's 4-1 victory over Tibet was anecdotal, as the match was so symbolic for both teams.

Since then, the large Arctic island has been trying to carve out a place for itself on the footballing planet. This goal is far from being achieved, as the Greenland Football Association was refused membership of FIFA in 2010. Sepp Blatter declared at the time: "According to the admission rules, for a soccer federation to be admitted it must come from an independent state recognized by the international community, i.e. the UN, in order to apply for membership of FIFA."[54] The case law of the Faroe Islands could not be invoked because more restrictive membership rules were established in 2004. However, since the handover of the FIFA presidency in 2015, the situation has changed, with Gibraltar, a British overseas territory claimed by Spain, and Kosovo, an internationally disputed state and non-member of the UN, now members of UEFA and FIFA.

There is another obstacle preventing Greenland from joining: infrastructure. Indeed, the "green island" cannot maintain a grass pitch due to the permafrost that envelops the territory. To remedy this, the Greenland authorities set up a partnership in 2015 with the Danish Football Federation to develop synthetic surfaces. Several

54. FIFA, "Greenland gripped by soccer fever", September 2010.

pitches have been installed across the country, including the national stadium in the capital Nuuk. This infrastructure is set to change, as the Greenlandic authorities are planning a new stadium, the Arktisk Stadion, with a capacity of over 3,000 spectators.

With the help of Denmark, Greenland has a good chance of joining UEFA and FIFA if this development continues in the right direction. Or why not CONCACAF, the North and Central American soccer confederation, given its proximity to the American continent and faster international success against less formidable teams? Greenland's handball and badminton federations have already turned to this option to give their athletes international stature and to compete against genuine national teams. Greenland's men's and women's handball teams have already taken part in several recent editions of the World Championships, pitting them against official national selections.

While we wait for Greenland to attempt to qualify for a soccer Euro, the "Polar Bears", as the team is known, are getting ready. The team is a member of CONIFA (see Chapter 12) and takes part in the Football Island Games, a sporting competition between the various Nordic islands, where the Greenlanders were finalists in 2017. In any case, the horizon seems to be brightening, as this move towards emancipation through soccer is supported by Denmark and other Scandinavian countries. Allan Hansen, President of the Danish Football Association, said at the 2017 UEFA Congress: "Greenland is currently in the pre-accession phase. I'm much more optimistic than I was five years ago."[55]

---

55. McGwin Kevin, "Greenland could soon be a step closer to joining the world of international soccer", *Arctic Now*, July 2017.

In any case, Greenland continues to attract international attention, and the next few years will be decisive for this country. Recent discoveries of rare-earth and uranium deposits will force Greenlanders to choose between economic sovereignty and environmental protection, and which path they wish to take on the road to independence.

21. Easter Island: Soccer to the Rescue of Rapa Nui

On April 6, 1722, the Dutch navigator Jakob Roggeveen discovered a piece of land lost in the middle of the Pacific Ocean: Easter Island. Famous for its Moai statues, the Rapa Nui people were gradually forgotten, exploited and forced into exile. To preserve their culture, the islanders have turned to soccer as a way out of their isolation.

Easter Island is a territory whose image is inseparable from that of the great moai statues. However, behind the postcard image, the indigenous Rapa Nui people have been fighting for years to have their rights respected. As activist Tuhiira Tucki Huke, a member of the Rapa Nui community, explains, "[i]t's difficult for a small people fighting all alone in the middle of the ocean for their rights, territory, land possession, identity, culture, intangible and tangible heritage," in a statement that follows 2018's broad media campaign for the restitution of Rapa Nui cultural heritage.

This people had been present on this lost island in the Pacific Ocean for hundreds of years. Navigator Jakob Roggeveen put an end to this isolation when he set out in search of a new spice trade route for the Dutch West India Company. The explorer set foot on the island on Easter Day, April 6, 1722, and named his discovery Easter Island. During the eighteenth century, despite the passage of Spanish and British ships and the famous French explorer La Pérouse, the island territory remained untouched by the lusts of the colonizing powers. As British cartographer James Cook summed up in his logs: "No nation will ever fight for the honor of having explored Easter Island, there is no island in the sea which offers less refreshment and convenience for navigation than this."[56] The island is indeed a hostile and, above all, isolated land. The nearest inhabited territories are Pitcairn Island, 2,075 km away, and the Chilean coast, over 3,500 km away.

As a result of this remoteness, the island wasn't really inhabited until the 13th century. At the same time, for example, as the arrival of the first settlers on the Hawaiian Islands. The first to set foot on Easter Island were known as the *Matamua,* Maori for "the first", and they founded the Rapa Nui culture. It was this name, Rapa Nui, that they gave to the island, which in the native language means "the navel of the world". The best-known aspect of this culture are the moai, immense statues with human figures, sculpted from tuff. These mysterious effigies are often blamed for the collapse of the indigenous people. The construction of these giants is said to have led to the drying up of the island's natural resources, resulting in "ecological suicide". The reality is far more complex. Clan wars and the construction of these statues should not obscure the Dantean environmental conditions of this territory, marked by earthquakes, droughts and tsunamis.

56. Cook James, *Livre de bord des voyages 1768-1779*, Erdmann, 2020.

It was above all the arrival of invaders that led to the eradication of the Rapa Nui population on the island. Numerous raids by slave traders from Peru reduced the local population from 2,500 in the early 18th century to just a hundred or so when the island was annexed by Chile in 1888. According to Emol Martín Lara, professor of history at the Silva Henríquez Catholic University, "in the 19th century, Peruvian ships would pick up islanders and bring them back to the country to be used as slaves".[57] The transition to Chilean sovereignty ushered in a new era, one that offered little hope for the few surviving Rapa Nui. They are parked in the reserve of Hanga Roa, the island's largest town, with the rest left to Chilean sheep breeders from the mainland.

It wasn't until 1966 that the locals were finally granted Chilean nationality and allowed to leave the reserve. This relative freedom was short-lived, however, as Chile became a dictatorship following Pinochet's coup d'état in 1973. With the return to democracy in 1989, the rights of the Rapa Nui evolved and were definitively recognized, thanks to the 1993 law on the protection of indigenous peoples. The situation on Easter Island gradually improved, particularly in demographic terms. From 1,200 inhabitants in 1982, the island has grown to over 7,500 today, around 60% of whom are of Rapa Nui origin. The development of infrastructure and Chile's opening up to the rest of the world have enabled the island to prosper, thanks in part to tourism.

These new prospects are prompting the indigenous people to demand greater autonomy. Easter Island is currently a province, which also includes the uninhabited island of Sala y Gómez,

57. "RAPA NUI: why is Easter Island changing its name?", *Le Petit Journal de Santiago*, August 2018.

located hundreds of kilometers to the east. This province enjoys "special regime" status, with powers similar to those of a regional government, but remains under the administration of the mainland region of Valparaiso. This situation is prompting local residents to demand greater autonomy. Above all, they want their culture and heritage, too often scorned, to be considered and restored. By way of example, only 14% of the island's land today belongs to the Rapa Nui, the rest to the Chilean state.

With this in mind, the local population is developing ways of showcasing its culture. Sport plays a key role. In particular, the island is turning to rugby. In 2016, it organized the "Seven of Rapa Nui", a tournament bringing together rugby 7s teams from French Polynesia, Easter Island and mainland Chile. Yet it is the round ball that offers the Rapa Nui people the opportunity to make their demands known to the world. Soccer is the island's most popular sport. The very first Rapa Nui Football Federation was set up in 1975, laying the foundations for a first team and, later, the creation of a local championship comprising 12 teams. The island is unique in having a team representing a selection of its best players, CF Rapa Nui, registered with the Chilean National Professional Football Association, which in theory allows it to play matches against other amateur and professional clubs in the country, as part of the federation's official competitions.

This "national team" made its first appearance outside the island in 1996, with a match at neighboring Juan Fernández. The result was a 5-3 victory. The turning point came a decade later, on August 5, 2009, with the first professional soccer match on Easter Island: a Chilean Cup match against Colo Colo, one of the country's most popular clubs. Roberto Araki Peña, a Rapa Nui player at the time, recalls: "We prepared for two months with Miguel Ángel

Gamboa, who played for Chile in the 1982 World Cup in Spain. We lasted 30 minutes, but they beat us 4-0. FIFA called it the match of the century. That's exactly how we lived it.[58] Despite the defeat, for Chile the match will serve to strengthen ties between the island and the mainland, as well as giving it international exposure, with the game being broadcast in several countries—Bolivia, Ecuador, Honduras and Argentina.

It's also an opportunity for the Rapa Nui people to showcase their culture. Before the match, they perform a traditional war dance called *hoko*, similar to the *haka* performed by New Zealand's All Blacks in rugby. FIFA, which described the match as the "match of the century", then helped the island to build up its soccer infrastructure. This was achieved with the construction of the 3,000-seat Rapa Nui de Hanga Roa stadium, inaugurated in 2014 in the presence of Brazilian legend Pelé and Chilean international Elias Figueroa. Pedro Edmunds, the local mayor at the time, said: "We're proud that a personality like Pelé came to such an important event for us. It gives visibility to a place like ours, which is one of the most isolated in the world, and immense joy to all the island's inhabitants."[59]

The Rapa Nui selection doesn't stop there, as it organizes the *Campeonato nacional de fútbol de Pueblos Originarios* (National Indigenous Peoples' Football Championship) with 7 other ethnic groups. It won the 2012 edition against the Mapuche team, an indigenous people from Chile and Argentina. The Easter Island team is also looking to forge links with Polynesian teams, as demonstrated by the Festival des îles tournament. For its first participation in 2018,

---

58. FIFA, "Football on Easter Island", April 2020.
59. Deplanque Sébastien, "Rapa Nui, l'autre île du soccer", *La Grinta*, April 2019.

Rapa Nui left with a respectable record of two wins, one draw and two defeats. The team's number 10, Tuki Muraccioli, says: "Some of us have been to Tahiti before, but this is the first time we've come as a team, as the Rapa Nui national soccer team in an official competition."[60] Following this success, the players return for the 2019 edition with a larger delegation, including a women's soccer and futsal team.

Lastly, the Rapa Nui national team joined CONIFA in 2019, which could enable it to compete against other international teams, pending eventual FIFA membership to take part in World Cup qualifiers. However, such a move seems unlikely given the island's relative autonomy and poor soccer infrastructure.

Things are moving in the right direction, however, as in 2018 the indigenous people obtained from Chile the renaming of Easter Island to Rapa Nui. The President of Chile, Sebastián Piñera, declared: "We want to make an act of historical reclamation and recognize the island's thousand-year-old origin." According to activist Tuhiira Tucki Huke, the reason the Chilean authorities are taking the Rapa Nui claims into their own hands is "to show compassion for the Rapa Nui people, it gets Chile talked about and it's good for the country's image, because Chile wants to position itself economically at international level"[61]. In fact, it helps to make people forget the harsh Chilean repression of Rapa Nui protests in the early 2010s.

Nevertheless, Easter Island remains a fragile territory. The island's economy relies heavily on tourism. With around 100,000

---

60. Kucsera Kevin, "Festival des îles 2018: Rapa Nui joins the party!", Tahitian Football Federation, April 2018.
61. Bordron Maïwenn, Chaverou Éric, "Île de Pâques : le combat du peuple Rapa Nui pour la restitution de son patrimoine culturel", *France Culture*, November 2018.

tourists a year, the influx of visitors is endangering the integrity of the island, already impacted by rising sea levels. This prompted the Chilean authorities to limit tourist activity in 2018, now at a standstill with the Covid-19 pandemic. Perhaps sport and soccer will be the ultimate levers enabling this isolated land to continue to exist.

22. Tuvalu Islands: Soccer Sounds the Alarm on Global Warming

At a time when rising sea levels are threatening the very existence of island territories more than ever, the Tuvalu Islands, a small archipelago in the Pacific Ocean, have decided to use soccer to raise awareness of global warming, which is threatening the very existence of their territory.

"No matter how much money you put on the table, it's not a valid reason not to do the right thing, which is to reduce your greenhouse gas emissions and not open new coal mines."[62] This is how Enele Sopoaga, former Prime Minister of Tuvalu, reacted to Australia's release of $300 million in September 2019 to help the Pacific islands. These territories are on borrowed time due to the consequences of global warming.

The Tuvalu Islands are a case in point. Lost in the immensity of the Pacific Ocean, the 8 atolls of this archipelago (*Tuvalu* means "8 together" in the local language) are home to just 12,000

62. Roy Ainge Eleanor, "One day we'll disapear: Tuvalu's sinking islands", *The Guardian*, May 2019.

inhabitants. These lands have the distinction of being one of the narrowest territories in the world, with the widest point measuring just 400 meters. However, these geographical constraints did not prevent the former British colony from becoming independent in 1978. In fact, the creation of the United Nations after the Second World War led to a long process of decolonization, particularly of the British colonies in the Pacific, and a move towards self-determination.

This recent independence quickly raised the question of economic sovereignty. With no natural resources of its own, the small archipelago had to turn to the sale of fishing licenses to emancipate itself and gain recognition as a country in its own right. It joined the United Nations on September 5, 2000, becoming the organization's 189th member. More surprisingly, this international recognition is also largely due to the Internet. One of Tuvalu's main sources of revenue is the national top-level domain, the famous ".tv", which brings in millions of dollars a year. However, this little-known financial windfall fails to highlight the special characteristics of this island territory.

The territory is classified by the United Nations as a "least developed country", due to its limited economic development potential, lack of resources and vulnerability to external environmental events. As a result, Tuvalu still relies heavily on an international sovereign wealth fund, financed by Australia and New Zealand. Tourism could be the answer to diversifying the country's economy, but poor infrastructure means that only around 2,000 visitors a year can reach them. Yet the archipelago needs international visibility to survive. Rising sea levels threaten the integrity of the country, which could be the first to be submerged within 50 years. The highest point of the islands is 4.6 meters above sea level, and there is a great risk that they will disappear. And this, even though other studies, dating from 2018, have pointed to the fact that these islands, geologically dynamic, are increasing in surface area and would adapt to changing sea levels. In any case, this dotted future does not delay the first consequences of climate change, with an increase in cyclones, droughts and other natural disasters.

The relocation of the population to New Zealand and Australia is, for the time being, not being considered by the Tuvaluan authorities. In 2015, Enele Sopoaga declared that "moving out of Tuvalu will not solve any climate change problem... If you move these people to the middle of industrialized countries, it will simply increase their consumption and increase greenhouse gas emissions".[63]

To develop, invest and put off the deadline, Tuvalu needs to reveal itself to the world. What better way than through sport to fly the flag at a major media sporting event?

This has been the case since 2007, when the Pacific islands were admitted to the International Olympic Committee (IOC). In 2008, this enabled them to take part in the world's most watched competition, the Olympic Games. Every four years since the Beijing Games, Tuvalu has sent a small delegation of one to three athletes. With its soccer team, Tuvalu has gained international recognition through sport.

Football is one of the country's most popular sports. One year after its independence, in 1979, the national team was already taking part in the South Pacific Games, and faced Tahiti in its first match on August 28, 1979. The match ended in a severe 18-0 defeat!

---

63. ROY Ainge Eleanor, "One day we'll disapear: Tuvalu's sinking islands", *The Guardian*, May 2019.

Three days later, however, the Tuvalu soccer team recorded its very first international victory against Tonga.

International matches are limited to this type of competition, as the archipelago is not part of the FIFA family, despite repeated requests since 1987. It has to be said that the world soccer organization has tightened the conditions for membership, particularly in terms of sports infrastructure. It is this last point that is lacking in Tuvalu. Without membership, there can be no participation in FIFA competitions, and hence in the World Cup. Even if it's true that, in the event of membership, it would still be a very long way to go to see Tuvalu take part in a World Cup. Since Australia's departure from the Oceania confederation, New Zealand has been the continent's leading football nation, collecting World Cup play-off tickets and Oceania championship titles. Since the early 2010s, Tuvalu have been investing in progress. Unfortunately, the team is unable to play at home, as the Tuvalu Sports Ground stadium is located on a clay and dented terrain. A solution has been found with their neighbors, Fiji, who are making their stadium and training center available to the Tuvalu Football Association—a temporary solution that is far from sufficient in FIFA's eyes.

But this doesn't stop the team from competing against other Pacific nations. Tuvalu even took part in the qualifiers for the 2010 World Cup! This was made possible by the fact that the 2007 South Pacific Games were considered the first stage in qualifying for the World Cup[64]. It could even be said that Tuvalu earned their first point in a World Cup qualifying match, as they drew with Tahiti

64. Frew Craig, "Tuvallu still dreams of joingin FIFA's world soccer family", *BBC Sport*, December 2013.

during the games. Viliamu Sekifu thus became the first Tuvaluan goalscorer in World Cup history.

Although the islanders lost most of their matches, their interest lay elsewhere: playing in an international competition and promoting their flag. The federation's limited financial resources and high travel costs forced the team to become less active in the late 2000s. It only came back thanks to partnerships set up with other countries. This has been the case since 2009, with the Dutch Support project, which forges close links between the Netherlands and Tuvalu, and results in the recruitment, in 2011, of a new Dutch coach, Foppe de Haan, currently Heerenveen's youth coach. In 2013, Tuvalu also took part in a three-month tour of the Netherlands to take on local teams.

Internationally, Tuvalu competes against teams other than its Oceanian neighbors, such as the United Koreans of Japan, Tamil Eelam and the Chagos Islands. This is made possible by the fact that the archipelago joined CONIFA in 2016. In fact, Tuvalu took part in the 2018 CONIFA World Cup in London, unfortunately losing three matches to Matabeleland, Padania and Sicily. Today, sport remains the Tuvaluans' best asset for publicizing the situation of their small nation and thus alerting to the issue of climate refugees and saving what can still be saved of our planet's biodiversity. As Enele Sopoaga said at COP21 in Paris in 2015: "Let's do it for Tuvalu, because if we save Tuvalu, we save the world."[65]

65. Roy Ainge Eleanor, "One day we'll disapear: Tuvalu's sinking islands", *The Guardian*, May 2019.

during the games. [illegible] thus became the first [illegible] goalkeeper in World Cup history.

[illegible]

Thanks

I'd particularly like to thank my brother Anthony for passing on his passion for soccer and geography to me as a child.

Thank you to my other half, Zoé, who supported and motivated me throughout this project with her advice, invaluable feedback and, above all, her love.

Thanks to my mother, Nadège, an unfailing support, whatever my projects and the obstacles to be overcome.

Thank you to Jean-Charles Gérard, my publisher, and Pascal Boniface for helping me bring this book project to fruition.

Thanks to my family and friends. In particular to the "club" of reviewers Florian, François, Geoffrey, Guillaume M., Guillaume C., Mathieu, Myriem, Romain and Sarah.

Thank you to all Football Club Geopolitics subscribers for your interest and support.

Finally, a thought for my grandmother, Pierrette, who I know will read these lines with emotion.

A tribute to my grandfather Aurelio, who was the first to tell me beautiful stories.

Bibliography and Sources

General works

Archambault Fabien, Beaud Stéphane, Gasparini William, *Le Football des nations: des terrains de jeu aux communautés imaginées,* Éditions de la Sorbonne, 2018.

Boniface Pascal, *Géopolitique du sport,* Armand Colin, 2014.

Boniface Pascal, *JO politiques,* Eyrolles, 2016.

Boniface Pascal, *L'Empire foot: comment le ballon rond a conquis le monde,* Armand Colin, 2018.

Correia Mickaël, *Une histoire populaire du soccer,* La découverte, 2018.

Dietschy Paul, *Histoire du soccer,* Perrin, 2010.

Ghemmour Chérif, *Terrain Miné, quand la politique s'immisce dans le soccer,* Hugo Sport, 2013.

Guégan Jean-Baptiste, *Géopolitique du sport, une autre explication du monde,* Bréal, 2017.

Wahl Alfred, *La Balle au pied. A History of Football,* Gallimard, 1990.

Chapter 1

Barcelo Laurent, "L'Europe des 52". L'Union Européenne de Football Association (UEFA)", *Guerres mondiales et conflits contemporains* n° 228, October 2007.

Gasparini William, *L'Europe du soccer, socio-histoire d'une construction européenne,* Presses universitaires de Strasbourg, 2017.

Germain Guillaume, *1960-2020: 60 ans d'Euro de soccer,* Jérôme Do Bentzinger éditeur, 2020.

Mouton Olivier, *Hors-Jeu. 22 soccer matches that made history,* Armand Colin, 2017.

Chapter 2

Germain Guillaume, *1960-2020: 60 ans d'Euro de soccer,* Jérôme Do Bentzinger éditeur, 2020.

Mouton Olivier, *Hors-Jeu. 22 soccer matches that made history,* Armand Colin, 2017.

- Internet sources

Goubin Thomas, "1964: L'Espagne se paye l'URSS", *So Foot,* May 2012.

Lukovic Viktor, "Un Euro 1960 entre Soviétiques et Franquistes", *Footballski,* April 2018.

Chapter 3

Germain Guillaume, *1960-2020: 60 ans d'Euro de soccer,* Jérôme Do Bentzinger éditeur, 2020.

Mouton Olivier, *Hors-Jeu. 22 soccer matches that made history,* Armand Colin, 2017.

Trégourès Loïc, *Football in the chaos of Yugoslavia,* Non Lieu, 2019.

- Internet sources

Chowdhury Saj, "Euro 1992: Denmark's fairytale", BBC Sport, May 2012.

Ghemmour Chérif, Pedro Alexandre, "Once upon a time Richard-Moller Niesen and Denmark 1992", *So Foot,* February 2014.

Chapter 4

Colovic Ivan, *Politics of Identity in Serbia,* NYU Press, 2002.

Riva Gigi, *The Last Penalty,* Seuil, 2016.

Trégourès Loïc, *Football in the chaos of Yugoslavia,* Non Lieu, 2019.

Wilson Jonathan, *Behind the Curtain. Travels In Eastern European Football,* Orion Publishing Co, 2006.

- Internet sources

Ghemmour Chérif, "The day Boban made his high kick", *So Foot,* May 2020

Chapter 5

Perryman Marc, *Ingerland: Travels With a Football Nation,* Simon & Schuster, 2006.

- Internet sources

Gibbons Michael, "The cultural resonance of Euro 96", *The Guardian,* July 2016.

Nakrani Sachin, "Golden goal: Paul Gascoigne for England *v.* Scotland (1996)", *The Guardian,* December 2014.

Wilson Richard, "20 years of regret from Euro 96 loss", *BBC Sport,* June 2016.

Chapter 6

- Internet sources

Boffey Daniel, “Mind our language: Bulgaria blocks North Macedonia’s EU path”, *The Guardian*, November 2020.

Perrier Fabien, “La Grèce reconnaît le nom de ‘Macédoine du Nord’”, *Le Temps*, January 2019.

Rédaction, “Football: a united North Macedonia celebrates its Euro qualification”, *Le Courrier des Balkans*, November 2020.

Chapter 7

Archambault Fabien, Beaud Stéphane, Gasparini William, *Le Football des nations: des terrains de jeu aux communautés imaginées*, Éditions de la Sorbonne, 2018.

AUBIN Lukas, La sportokratura sous Vladimir Poutine, Editions Bréal, 2021

- Internet sources

Boy Louis, “Four years after annexation by Russia, the slow decline of soccer in Crimea”, *Franceinfo*, June 2018.

Candau Adrien, “Crimée, la balle dans le pied”, *So Foot*, June 2018.

Mosko Alexei, “Crimea wants to become a soccer nation in its own right”, *Russia Beyond*, November 2016.

Chapter 8

Trégourès Loïc, *Football in the chaos of Yugoslavia*, Non Lieu, 2019.

Lefevre Florian, “Fadil Vokrri”, *So Foot*, June 2020.

- Internet sources

AMES Nick, “Kosovo’s dream team is ready to inspire a more hopeful future”, *The Guardian*, September 2019.

Chapter 9

- Internet sources

MCELWEE Molly, “The inside story of how Gibraltar has stunned soccer”, *The Telegraph*, November 2018.

MONTAGUE James, “Gibraltar moves closer to soccer independence”, *New York Times*, May 2013.

PENALBA SOTORRIO Mercedes, “Gibraltar: a history of ill will over the Rock”, *The Conversation*, April 2017.

Chapter 10

- Internet sources

AFP, “Ligue Europa: à Bakou, le sport en vitrine du régime”, May 2019.

COLLIN Jean-Christophe, “De retour du front, les footballeurs du Haut-Karabakh retrouvent le terrain”, *L’Équipe*, December 2020.

DOYLE Paul, “Why did UEFA hand Azerbaijan hosting rights for the Europa League final?”, *The Guardian*, May 2019.

Chapter 11

- Internet sources

DUEZ Julien, “We were at the CONIFA World Cup final”, *So Foot*, June 2018.

MENETIER Denis, “Comté de Nice, Ruthénie subcarpatique, Abkhazie... bienvenue à la CONIFA, l’antichambre de la FIFA”, *France TV Sport*, February 2021.

Weeks Jonny, "The Alternative World Cup", *The Guardian,* June 2018.

Chapter 12

- Internet sources

Dowling Tim, "The World Cup sides you've never heard of", *The Guardian,* June 2008.

Kejonen Olle, "1985: Sápmis första landskamp", *Sverige Radio,* August 2015.

Pave Linn Margrete, "Nytt Samisk fotballforbund—FA Sápmi", *NRK Sápmi,* May 2014.

Chapter 13

- Internet sources

Anner Niels, "Triumph von ein paar Freunden" NZZ, October 2016

Destine Eric, "Åland: cet "État dans l'État" au sein de l'UE qui intrigue les indépendantistes", RTBF, June 2019

Willis Craig, Hughes Will, Bobr Sergiusz, "ECMI Minorities Blog. National and Linguistic Minorities in the Context of Professional Football across Europe". ECMI. June 2023.

Chapter 14

- Internet sources

Chadband Ian, "San Marino hero who humiliated England", *Evening Standard,* March 2003.

Hughes Rebecca Ann, "A Historic Season for the world's worst national soccer team", *Forbes,* December 2020.

Pauluzzi Valentin, interview with Andy Sellva, *So Foot,* March 2015.

Chapter 15

GHEMMOUR Chérif, *Terrain Miné, quand la politique s'immisce dans le soccer*, Hugo Sport, 2013.

KAPUŚCIŃSKI Ryszard, *The Soccer War*, Granta Books, 1990.

- Internet sources

CALMARD Diego, "Il y a 50 ans, le match Honduras-Salvador déclenchait la 'guerre du foot'", *Médiapar* "blogs", June 2019.

Chapter 16

- Internet sources

AUBRY Émilie, "Hong Kong : la fin des libertés ? Une leçon de géopolitique", *Arte* ("Le dessous des cartes"), December 2020.

DE CHANGY Florence, "À Hongkong, la loi de sécurité imposée par la Chine met brutalement fin à une exception démocratique", *Le Monde*, July 2020.

ROSS Donald, "China National Team. The 5.19 incident: China's doomed attempt to qualify for Mexico'86," *WideEastFootball.net*, October 2017.

WOOD Chris, "When Hong Kong beat China in a World Cup qualifier 32 years ago, and riots that followed", *South China Morning Post*, May 2017.

Chapter 17

GHEMMOUR Chérif, *Terrain Miné, quand la politique s'immisce dans le soccer*, Hugo Sport, 2013.

- Internet sources

BRIGAND Maxime, "Argentina-England 1986, le caprice de Dieu", *So Foot*, November 2020.

CARLIN John, “England vs Argentina—A history”, *The Guardian*, May 2002.

CAVALONNE Elena, “With Brexit, uncertainty looms over the future of the Falkland Islands”, *Euronews*, January 2021.

GARRIC Audrey, “Les Malouines, trente ans de conflit irrésolu”, *Le Monde*, April 2012.

Chapter 18

BLAKE Heidi and CALVERT Jonathan, *The Ugly Game: The Qatari Plot to Buy the World Cup*, Simon&Chuster, 2016.

GUÉGAN Jean-Baptiste, *Géopolitique du sport, une autre explication du monde*, Bréal, 2017.

- Internet sources

CHADWICK Simon, “Why Saudi Arabia won't buy an English soccer team”, *Policy Forum*, February 2020.

CONN David, “Qatar 2022: £40 a week to build the World Cup stadiums”, *The Guardian*, November 2018.

GOMEZ Carole, “Le sport, un levier d'influence pour l'Arabie saoudite”, RFI interview, January 2020.

LE MAGOARIEC Raphaël, “La stratégie du Qatar pour devenir un grand du soccer”, *Orient XXI*, November 2016.

MCINTYRE Niamh, PATTISSON Pete, “Revealed: 6,500 migrant workers have died in Qatar since World Cup awarded”, *The Guardian*, February 2021.

ZIDAN Karim, “Sportswashing: how Sauda Arabia lobbies the US's largest sports bodies”, *The Guardian*, September 2019.

Chapter 19

Correia Mickaël, *Une histoire populaire du soccer,* La découverte, 2018.

Ghemmour Chérif, *Terrain Miné, quand la politique s'immisce dans le soccer,* Hugo Sport, 2013.

- Internet sources

Rouaba Ahmed, "The incredible story of Algeria's 'independence dribblers,'" *BBC Afrique,* May 2018.

Chapter 20

- Internet sources

Knox Tomos, "The unlikely success stroye of soccer on the massive island of Greenland", *These Football Times,* October 2014.

McGwin Kevin, "Greenland could soon be a step closer to joining the world of international soccer", *Arctic Now,* July 2017.

Petite Simon, "Groenland et îles Féroé : au Nord, l'indépendance à petits pas", *Le Temps,* April 2018.

Editor, "Football in Greenland", *Nordisk Football,* October 2017.

Smith Rory, "Soccer at the Edge of the World", *The New York Times,* September 2019.

Ward Tom, "The inside story of Greenland's one-week soccer season", *Red Bull,* November 2019.

Chapter 21

- Internet sources

Bordron Maïwenn, Chaverou Éric, "Île de Pâques : le combat du peuple Rapa Nui pour la restitution de son patrimoine culturel", *France Culture,* November 2018.

DEPLANQUE Sébastien, “Rapa Nui, l’autre île du soccer”, *La Grinta*, April 2019.

FIFA, “Football on Easter Island”, April 2020.

KUCSERA Kevin, “Festival des îles 2018: Rapa Nui joins the party!”, Tahitian Football Federation, April 2018.

LONG Gilden, “Easter Island has soccer début”, *BBC News*, August 2009.

“RAPA NUI: why is Easter Island changing its name?”, *Le Petit Journal de Santiago*, August 2018.

Chapter 22

- Internet sources

BISOGNO Dominic José, “What Tuvalu and Kiribati’s growing inclusion could mean for both nations and the OFC”, *These Football Times*, June 2020.

FREW Craig, “Tuvallu still dreams of joingin FIFA’s world soccer family”, *BBC Sport*, December 2013.

ROY Ainge Eleanor, “One day we’ll disapear: Tuvalu’s sinking islands”, *The Guardian*, May 2019.

Table of Contents

Part Two: Beyond Europe

www.ingramcontent.com/pod-product-compliance
Lightning Source LLC
La Vergne TN
LVHW010555160826
845677LV00013B/3132

* 9 7 8 2 3 1 5 0 2 1 6 2 8 *